NEIGHBORHOOD MAPPING

HOW TO MAKE YOUR CHURCH INVALUABLE TO THE COMMUNITY

DR. JOHN FUDER

MOODY PUBLISHERS

CHICAGO

© 2014 by
JOHN FUDER

Scripture quotations are taken from the New American Standard Bible˚,
Copyright © 1960, 1962, 1963, 1968, 1971, 1972, 1973, 1975, 1977, 1995 by The
Lockman Foundation. Used by permission. (www.Lockman.org)

Edited by Ginger Kolbaba
Cover design: Studio Gearbox
Interior design: Smartt Guys design
Cover image: Chad Baker / Photodisc

Library of Congress Cataloging-in-Publication Data
Fuder, John.
 Neighborhood mapping : how to make your church invaluable to the community
/ Dr. John Fuder.
     pages cm
 Includes bibliographical references.
 ISBN 978-0-8024-1134-1
 1. Communities--Religious aspects--Christianity. I. Title.
 BV625.F83 2014
 254'.4--dc23
                          2013045930

We hope you enjoy this book from Moody Publishers. Our goal is to
provide high-quality, thought-provoking books and products that connect truth
to your real needs and challenges. For more information on other books
and products written and produced from a biblical perspective, go to
www.moodypublishers.com or write to:

Moody Publishers
820 N. LaSalle Boulevard
Chicago, IL 60610

1 3 5 7 9 10 8 6 4 2

Printed in the United States of America

Praise for *Neighborhood Mapping*

The needs in underprivileged communities are too often misunderstood and neglected, resulting in devastating impact upon the already poor and marginalized. *Neighborhood Mapping* by Dr. John Fuder is an engaging, practical tool available to assist workers in the field to better understand the communities they are involved with, and I highly recommend it as an easy-to-use resource to those who care about ministry to "the least of these."

> —**DR. WESS STAFFORD**, President emeritus of Compassion International
> Author of *Too Small to Ignore* and *Just a Minute*

I count it a privilege to endorse this book written by a man who loves the Lord but who also loves the great city of Chicago with its sprawling neighborhoods, broken social systems, and well-known reputation for criminal activity! John's heart beats for this city, for its families, its churches, and its children. Rather than run from these challenges, he is attracted to them, believing that God can be counted on to work mightily where the needs are greatest. At last we can benefit from John's expertise, so we can better understand our particular city and minister without fear, knowing that God Himself loves the cities of the world. In short, this book is a gift to all who have a burden for the great and growing urban areas of the world that long to be understood, loved, and transformed with an authentic gospel witness.

> —**DR. ERWIN W. LUTZER**, Senior Pastor, The Moody Church

Today most Christians are not short on a desire to impact city neighborhoods for Christ. Our only challenge is that our good intentions are soon sabotaged by our inability to know and understand the neighborhood dynamics in which we are trying to work. This "pin-the-tail-on-the-donkey" approach to neighborhood ministry sometimes is more harmful than helpful. So a big-time "thanks" to my friend John Fuder who helps us take the blindfold off so we can minister with eyes wide open toward effective outcomes.

> —**DR. JOSEPH STOWELL**, President, Cornerstone University

I've had the privilege of working with my friend Dr. John Fuder for close to twenty-five years to make the gospel relevant in under-resourced communities. It is with great enthusiasm that I recommend his new book, *Neighborhood Mapping*, to anyone who has a heart for seeing their communities impacted by the good news of Jesus Christ.

> —**NOEL CASTELLANOS**, CEO,
> Christian Community Development Association

A naval officer once told me "theory without practice is dangerous, practice without theory is deadly." Dr. Fuder has street cred. As many churches launch into "inner-city" kinds of ministries, they will save time and frustration learning from Dr. Fuder's experience. Thanks, John, for helping us share Christ in complex places.

> —**DR. MICHAEL EASLEY**, Teaching Pastor, Fellowship Bible Church
> Former president, Moody Bible Institute

When I first moved to Chicago over nine years ago the first person many told me I needed to meet with was John Fuder. I was told over and over again what an insightful and compassionate man he is. After meeting with him many times over the years I can only say—those were understatements. John loves the city and sees the city through a compassionate, hospitable, and gospel grid. He has been able to make alliances when others have not. He is trusted where many others are seen with a cautious eye. He wades in where many are hesitant.

> —**JACKSON CRUM**, Lead Pastor, Park Community Church

I cannot think of anyone more qualified to develop a gospel-centered community analysis format than Dr. John Fuder. As a graduate student in his class at Moody Theological Seminary, his teaching transformed my spiritual life. The same passion he demonstrated in the classroom is clearly reflected in the pages of this book.

Without a doubt, this guide will provide users with a tool to effectively create and transform spiritual community ministry. I commend Dr. Fuder for his continued commitment to the cause of urban ministry.

> —**BERLEAN M. BURRIS, PhD**, Professor (retired),
> Moody Theological Seminary

If you long to see urban churches unified and God strategically moving through them, Dr. Fuder has created the text to aid in that vision. If you are a community activist, church planter, pastor, or lay leader in the city, this handbook is a necessity. God wants you to know your neighborhood, and with this Dr. Fuder has compiled all the tools needed to bring understanding and depth of knowledge to your context.

> —**CANDY GIBSON**, National Recruiting Director, World Impact

They say the world is flat and that we are all one big interconnected community, yet many churches still know little about their own communities. Community analysis as prescribed in this book will help ensure more effective outreach and better stewardship of kingdom resources for reaching your community.

> —**STEVE ROA**, Director of Strategic Partnerships,
> US Center of World Missions

As I read through this wonderfully crafted tool for effective community analysis, the recurring thought in the back of my mind was "if only." "If only" this well thought-out professional tool was available to my coworkers and me when we were serving overseas, how much better we would have understood and ministered to the people to whom we were sent. This manual is applicable anywhere in the world, and I especially encourage those working cross-culturally to make systematic use of it.

> —**DR. MARVIN NEWELL**, Senior Vice President, Missio Nexus

John Fuder has given us a helpful resource for analyzing and engaging our communities. This user-friendly guide uses the tools of ethnography to learn about our communities but with a thorough integration with spirituality and how God sees our community. This will be useful for students learning about engaging the city, as well as churches that are looking for guidance as they learn and reach out around them. The appendices are a wonderful bonus, containing helpful tools and surveys. I expect to use this often.

> —**DR. JUDE TIERSMA WATSON**, InnerCHANGE,
> Associate Professor of Urban Mission, Fuller Seminary

Truly here is a tool I wish I had twenty years ago in our ministry. *Neighborhood Mapping* not only inspires the concept of incarnational presence in the city, but shows us how to do it well. Anyone who seeks to understand the life and soul of their neighborhood and city will want to make this book a part of their toolbox. Thank you, Doc Fuder, for another gift to all of us who are laboring to love the city.

> —**BRAD STANLEY**, Director, YWAM Chicago
> Author, *Finding God in the City*

John, you sold me at the table of contents! Every city movement lead team needs your question-prompted process for analyzing their communities in real-time discovery rather than mere theory. The city movements I coach will welcome this new resource because it equips them to answer critical questions of how to examine neighborhoods and exegete the unique and changing culture of communities.

Neighborhood Mapping is a strategic approach that is perfectly suited to assist the whole church to show and tell the whole gospel to the whole city. Your use of Scripture is a refreshing juxtaposition of biblical truth and practical action steps, a field guide for both fresh thought and best practice leaders. Based on a lifetime of scholarly study and street-level service, it is up-to-date and state-of-the-art. On behalf of many city reachers, collaborative enterprises, and outward focused pastors and prayer leaders, "Bravo and thank you!"

> —**PHIL MIGLIORATTI**, National Coordinator,
> Loving Our Communities to Christ / COO, Mission America Coalition

CONTENTS

FOREWORD

Cities across America were exploding when I moved into inner-city Chicago in 1965. Driven by two simultaneous social revolutions—the long-festering civil rights movement and the anti-Vietnam War movement—these uprisings blended into what an official commission termed "The Police Riots" at the 1968 Democratic Convention in Chicago.

At their best, revolutions force us to become informed and to set our priorities. Looking back on that era, I contend that Darwin, Marx, and Freud were a stiff intellectual breeze for me at the university, but nothing in my experience compared to the failure of the evangelical churches, schools, and mission societies that had nurtured and educated me until then. We called it "white fright and white flight." It seemed as if all the urban churches that sang, "red and yellow, black and white; they are precious in his sight," ran the moment they showed up in their communities or at their kids' schools. Many churches, made famous as supporters of missions overseas, fled amidst the opportunity of missions here at home.

As we settled into our Chicago home, my wife and I made three vows: First, we would stay, raise our two preschool kids in the inner city, and enroll them in the same public schools where the kids on our street would go. Second, we would set out to study Chicago, to see if we could understand and eventually love it, corruption and all. Third, we knew we had to find a theology as big as huge cities. I give witness to the sad fact that I had already graduated from a great Bible institute, a superb evangelical university, and was a student in a highly regarded evangelical seminary, but had never had a course in cities of Scripture, or urban church history or ministry. Chicago became my world-class lab for thirty-five years, and now our kids serve in Chicago, Washington DC, and on a Native American reservation.

It was not long before I began to see a new generation of city-focused leaders emerge in Chicago, strong people such as Wayne Gordon at Lawndale and John Fuder at Moody Graduate School. This new breed took to cities as ducks to water. They thrived on the social, racial, and religious pluralism. Like me, they read Scripture as an urban book, noticing in texts such as Psalm 107 that it is God's great idea to bring nations into urban neighborhoods. The frontiers of mission shifted from across oceans to across streets in cities on six continents, and that ministry now must be 24/7 with day ministries and night ministries in all languages and with all sorts of new outreach and discipleship strategies. Like hospitals, police, and supermarkets, churches must get in touch with this reality. While folks like Wayne took the Christian Community Development Association (CCDA) and went national to recruit and train these young, radical, missional folks, "Doc" John Fuder was lighting a fire under his students at Moody in ways that led a faculty colleague to describe him as "the Michael Jordan of our faculty."

John was taking his students all over Chicago, introducing them to ministries of significance, and like me, had discovered that the Holy Spirit was alive and well, and teaching churches of all colors and denominations new ways of communicating the gospel. John met me one morning in a restaurant, grabbed a paper napkin, and outlined the first draft of his monumental book, *A Heart for the City*, which documented what he and his students had found. Ten years later in 2009, John partnered with Noel Castellanos, colleague of Wayne Gordon and John Perkins in CCDA, to finally publish *A Heart for the Community: New Models for Urban and Suburban Ministry.*

Clearly by then, John and others discovered that suburbs were no longer the "escape from the city, but the extension of it," so there is no place to hide from cities. Suburbs are often the most radically pluralized and rapidly changing communities in America today. Now, John has taken his learning into cities beyond Chicago, in some ways not unlike what happened to me after 1980 when I was asked to go global. But John is much more organized and systematic than I was. He has a lot of new tools for helping people examine neighborhoods, and for helping churches "scratch where communities itch." When I read his stuff it's like going to school again. One fantasy for me now is to imagine I will show up in a city where he is working with folks, to sit with them, and learn from John.

It is a personal joy to commend *Neighborhood Mapping* to you, for the cause of global urban mission. Let John help you and your church or ministry get in touch with your community. I conclude with a farewell, heard so often from the lips of our late, great Chicago friend and fellow minister, Bill Leslie of LaSalle Street Church: "Thanks, John, for all you do for so many in the kingdom!"

RAY BAKKE
The Center for Global Urban Leadership, Seattle
Chancellor, Union University of California
Professor, Bethel Seminary Hong Kong

PREFACE

A sling in David's hand toppled a giant. The jawbone of a donkey in Samson's hand took out a thousand enemies. A laptop can make a grease monkey look like a mechanical engineer. A GPS makes a New York City cab driver look like a genius. The right tool in the right hands can produce amazing results.

That's what John Fuder has given us in this handbook. *Neighborhood Mapping* is a tool for on-the-ground practitioners who want to increase their effectiveness in community ministry. Uncomplicated enough to guide new recruits yet sufficiently sophisticated to enhance the veteran's arsenal, this biblically based workbook provides structure for exploring a complex urbanizing world. More than thirty years of practical experience in the urban context—teaching as well as ministering—has prepared John to create a well-designed tool that not only provides a portal for exploration but accelerates the learning process.

And yet *Neighborhood Mapping* is more than an instrument for gathering and processing data. To be sure, good data is important to properly understand a rapidly changing world. Demographic shifts, economic trends, educational standards—these and a score of other quantifiable measures are certainly significant to gaining an accurate picture of context. But community is about more than baseline data. It is also about the less quantifiable aspects: relationships, spiritual life, and unique personalities. *Neighborhood Mapping* takes all these factors into account and provides a plan for sensitively, comprehensively navigating both the visible as well as the more hidden realities of urban life.

Follow this guide and you will be surprised and delighted at the insights, even expertise, you will gather in the process. There's nothing like a good tool to enhance one's capacity.

BOB LUPTON
President, FCS Urban Ministries
A forty-year urban veteran

INTRODUCTION: HOW RELEVANT IS YOUR CHURCH?

Inner-city missionary Mark Van Houten wrote, "No matter how adept an exegete a theologian is . . . it is all for naught if he does not also understand his contemporary audience well enough to lead them to a correct understanding."[1] In a world that is constantly moving and changing, it is imperative that the church not only know how to interpret the Bible but also how to engage with and adapt to those for whom the gospel message is addressed. When we exegete a community, we draw meaning from it. We discover the underlying history, context, and culture of that place and its people.

According to the Pew Forum on Religion and Public Life, 214 million people all over the world moved out of their country of origin. Of those, 20 percent (42.8 million) moved to the United States.[2] In Chicagoland alone, more than 1.6 million of the population is foreign born.[3] In 2011, more than 52 percent of the world's population was urban (3.63 billion people).[4] In order for God's people to be an active presence in their neighboring communities and be engaged with those needs around them, they have to be increasingly aware of that audience: their hopes, their dreams, and their needs.

Many years ago I did my doctoral work in "skid row" in Los Angeles. The primary assignment in my first class was to build a relationship with a person from a culture different from our own and then develop a ministry strategy to reach that person. Since my wife and I had recently moved to the area, I contacted a close friend, who lived on the edge of "skid row" and did ministry there. He encouraged me to connect with a man he knew as Green Eyes. Green Eyes lived in a refrigerator-sized cardboard box down the street from my friend. He felt Green Eyes would be perfect for me to get to know, because he was deeply marginalized, and he also knew everything happening in that community and could let me into his world.

So on a Saturday morning in late January, I approached his "home" and knocked tentatively on the top of his box. Out popped his head and he voiced a number of words at me I won't repeat here! I introduced myself and explained that I was studying to be a teacher in Chicago and that I wanted to learn about his community and life so that I could take that understanding to my students. Then I asked him to teach me about life on the streets, if he would be my "teacher." I'll never forget the look in his eyes. It blew him away that a white boy, a total stranger, would ask him to school me. Over the next several months he introduced me to everyone he knew and told me about his life. And eventually he became a Christ-follower.

I realized I didn't know Green Eyes's world and had to take the posture of a learner. And I longed for my students to have tears of compassion and awareness of the needs of broken people. The only way that was going to happen was if God took me through the same process. In a sense what I did in the skid row community of Los Angeles was community analysis. From my time spent with Green Eyes, I was able to understand better the needs of his community and strategize how best to minister to them, right where they were.

Analyzing our communities enables us to explore and rediscover our surroundings. Once we make sense of our context, we can begin to "diagnose" needs and apply the proper "dose" of the gospel to meet those opportunities. Community analysis is the methodology and vehicle to rediscover our missional mandate in the church: to proclaim and demonstrate the gospel. The focus shifts from those inside the building to those outside—it is about the people we seek to reach. We must help our people see that "neighbor love" is an important part of following Jesus, and that moves us to find ways to know our neighbors in order to minister to and serve them well.

Neighborhood Mapping helps us apply what we learn, within the context of Scripture, in tangible ways. Neighborhoods are changing as people are constantly moving in and out of our cities. Ethnic and religious diversity is all around us. The work of community analysis is a task we must continue to do over and over again. It is never a "one and done" thing.

Just as we share our faith, make disciples, and consistently pray, it is equally important to "exegete," or "read," our audience, in order to draw meaning from them. This requires that we push the body of Christ to understand those around them and provide the practical skills to know how to do so.

In this book we look at how to reach our communities and make our churches invaluable to those neighborhoods, through the process of community analysis. Community analysis is a four-step process; it's what I call the 4Ss: *supplication, stakeholders, surveys,* and *stories.*

Supplication or prayer is the first step. Before we do anything else in our communities, we seek, individually and corporately, God's direction and leading. We also practice prayer-walking to see our neighborhoods up close, which gives us a feel for who lives there and allows God to draw our attention to certain needs and issues residing there.

The second S or step is to focus on stakeholders, or people within the community with whom we can partner or network, such as neighborhood leaders, churches/ministries, social services, or schools or businesses. When I worked in Los Angeles, my stakeholder, or gatekeeper, was Green Eyes. As an insider he knew the neighborhood as no one else and got me introduced into places I could have never gone on my own.

The third S or step is to administer surveys. Through question-naires and gathering focus groups, we get a stronger idea of our neighbors' felt needs, worldviews, and attitudes toward church and faith in general.

And finally, the fourth S is to gather the stories we hear through those questionnaires and interviews and put them into ethnogra-phies, or case studies, to get a fuller picture of our neighbors so that we can better minister and reach out to them.

Community analysis involves a "what," "when," "why," "who," "where," and "how" strategy of postures and practices. In this book we will discover each phase through a step-by-step plan, guided by prayer and biblical principles, toward practical, hands-on opportu-nities to engage our communities.

Community analysis has been a key component in my personal ministry for more than thirty years, inspired by God and informed by Scripture. It is a biblically based applied research approach that helps churches and organizations understand the unmet needs and untapped resources of a defined area and implement data-driven practical initiatives to transform that community.

Whether you are a church planter looking to start a ministry in a new area, a pastor or layperson in a church that feels irrelevant to the community, or an individual who wants to know how to better reach those around you, this community analysis handbook will help you and your ministry discover the needs of the area and give ideas of how to meet those needs.

You'll also find appendices that will give you more specifics, such as survey templates, what a finished ethnography looks like, and other useful information.

I encourage you to walk through this handbook with a group and invite members of your church, organization, or community to join you in the journey. First and foremost, this is an opportunity to build relationships, develop a heart of compassion, and share the gospel in fresh and unique ways.

Chapter 1

ONE CHURCH'S SUCCESS STORY: ADAPTING TO THE GROWING LATINO COMMUNITY

Our neighborhoods are in a continual state of change. God is sending the nations to our cities and as Christ-followers embedded in local churches we are, at times, overwhelmed in how to respond. Pastor David Potete, one of my former graduate students and longtime friend and ministry comrade in the Belmont-Cragin (Bel-Cragin) neighborhood on Chicago's Northwest Side, talked to me recently about the learning curve in working with his church to engage the community. His journey serves as a blueprint for us as we study and serve our changing communities. Here is his story.

I knew the importance of understanding demographics and the need to know the community the church is trying to reach. So when I and a few others planted Northwest Community Church in Chicago in 1991, I spent $600 on a demographic study of our neighborhood. But even with that knowledge, I had no idea the stunning value exegeting our community would have on the life of our church. In 2005 as part of my graduate studies, I took Dr. Fuder's class on community analysis. While it gave me a better understanding of what it means to be a student of my community, it only paved the way to the greater firsthand knowledge that came a year later when Dr. Fuder asked me if his graduate class could partner with our church to do a community analysis of our neighborhood.

Of course, I said yes. I knew I would learn more about the area I served. I met with the graduate students, discussed the neighborhood as I understood it, and worked with the class to develop a survey. The experience was informative and enlightening, since it challenged me to articulate my perceptions in a way I had not previously been forced to.

We surveyed the neighborhood, the grad class tabulated the results, and presented a booklet with several suggestions to our church. Though I was grateful for the experience, I didn't expect some great insight that would revolutionize our church.

At the time Northwest Community Church was 85 percent Caucasian, 10 percent Latino, and 5 percent African-American. Being in the predominantly Latino neighborhood of Bel-Cragin, it was obvious to everyone that we needed to become more Spanish-speaking in our services. We made some effort, but admittedly, it was not very intentional. And not very effective. The most we usually did was to occasionally sing a song or read a Scripture in Spanish.

> **THOUGH WE KNEW THE DEMOGRAPHICS BY EXPERIENCE, TO SEE IT IN BLACK AND WHITE ON THE PAGE WAS CRITICAL.**

When our church was presented with the community analysis report, however, we felt as if it were a smack in the face. It helped us understand our community as we never had before. It clarified where we were. And it made it crystal clear to us where we needed to go.

Even simply pointing out the demographic makeup of Bel-Cragin in the report was eye-opening. Though we knew the demographics by experience, to see it in black and white on the page was critical. The report's recommendations made it clear we must be bilingual. Community analysis gave us insights that truly revolutionized our church!

With the report and our new knowledge and understanding of our neighborhood, the first thing we did was to revisit and develop a theology of the nations for our church. We already had that kind of theology for our international missions, but it was lacking for missions around our block. We studied passages in Scripture and concluded that our mandate to make disciples starts right on our street! We now hold the conviction that we are to be a truly multiethnic, multicultural, and multilingual church. Part of that conviction is that we now hold bilingual services with Spanish and English combined in the same service.

We realized that if we wanted to serve and reach our community—as our name suggests—we had to make deliberate and intentional changes. In fact, our associate pastor, Gowdy Cannon, took the results so seriously that he traveled to Peru for a month to immerse himself in Spanish. We developed a translation team and began translating our flyers, bulletins, website, and worship slides into Spanish. We also invested in an FM transmission system to provide live translation through headphones.

Next we looked at our sanctuary's setup. The chairs faced the stage at the front of the sanctuary. One Sunday we moved the chairs into four sections with each section facing the center of the room. Instead of standing on the stage to preach, I stood in the center of the floor. When I was seated, I looked directly at my brothers and sisters worshiping. The first time I saw the joy of my Latino church family worshiping in their heart language confirmed to me that what we were doing was pleasing to God and a blessing to others. We now rearrange the chairs for this type of setup several times a year.

We still have a long way to go. Our attendance is now about 35 percent Latino, 5 percent African-American, 50 percent Caucasian, and a smattering of everything else.

There is no doubt in my mind we have become more of the church God wants us to be as a result of engaging in community analysis. And we are committed to reengaging in that type of analysis every few years to stay on track.

I thought I knew my community, and I did to a degree. However, the process of community analysis clarified, crystalized, and truly changed our approach to fulfilling the Great Commission in our neighborhood.

Armed with knowledge, understanding, and the Holy Spirit's guidance, we too can go out into our communities to meet people where they are and introduce them to the gospel. Let's get started.

TOP TEN TIPS TO EXEGETE A CULTURE[1]

As we start unpacking exactly what neighborhood mapping, or community analysis, is and how to do it, let the following step-by-step process guide your journey. We'll go more in-depth with each of these in the following chapters.

1. Go as a Learner

Assume a position to understand, not judge the neighborhood. This requires humility, persistence, and the courage to push past your fears. An accepting and inquisitive posture can open doors into another culture. Linguist and missions author Betty Sue Brewster's steps of cultural learning is helpful here: Come as a learner, find ways to serve, seek to form friendships, weave God's story into their story, and bathe everything in prayer.[2]

2. Seek Out an "Informant"

Find an individual who is a gatekeeper, an insider, a "[person] of peace" (Luke 10:6). This is someone who will let you into his lifestyle or subculture. He is an expert who can teach you about his journey as "lived experience." She is a model (albeit imperfect!) of another belief or practice and can connect you to that world.

3. Build a Relationship

As much as you can, be a "participant observer"[3] in that person's life, culture, and activities. A relationship, growing into a friendship, is key because in it a "trust-bond"[4] is formed, and trust is the collateral of cross-cultural ministry. In the process, God is at work to break your heart for that community (see Matt. 9:13; Luke 13:34).

4. Use an Interview Guide

You may not always "stay on script," but it is helpful to work from an outline. You could apply the same categories already provided and then adapt the questions (see appendix 1) within them to meet your specific needs.

5. Analyze Your Data

Depending on the formality of your community analysis, you will in all likelihood end up with some form of "field notes." A crucial step, often neglected, is to examine your data for holes, patterns, or hooks. What missing pieces could your informant fill in? What interests, activities, or values are recurrent themes? Is there anything you could use to enter your informant's world more deeply?

6. Filter through a Biblical Worldview

What Scriptures speak to the information you are discovering? What does the Bible say about the activities, lifestyles, and beliefs you are exegeting or reading in your neighborhood? What would Jesus do, or have you do, in response to the needs? A biblical framework is your strongest platform on which to mobilize your church/ministry/school to action.

7. Expand into the Broader Community

Your informant can act as a "culture broker" to give you entry into the additional lifestyles and subcultures within the broader community. As you learn to "read your audience" (become "streetwise") and develop credibility in the neighborhood, you can leverage those relational contacts into greater exposure and deeper familiarity with the needs in your area.

8. Network Available Resources

As your awareness of the community grows, you will invariably feel overwhelmed by all there is to do, missionally speaking! You do not have to reinvent the wheel. Is anyone else working with that audience? Can you partner with another church, ministry, or agency? With whom can you share and gather resources and information?

9. Determine What God Is Calling You to Do

With your newly acquired knowledge about your community, what do you do now? Plant a church? Start a new ministry? Refocus your current programs? Much of your response will depend upon your personnel and resources. But you are now poised to do relevant, kingdom-building work in your community.

10. Continually Evaluate, Study, Explore

Our hope in Christ is firm, but everything and everyone around us is in constant motion. Is your neighborhood changing (again)? Who is God bringing to your community now? Is your church or ministry responsive to those opportunities? Are you winsome, relevant, engaging? We must always ask these questions, in every generation, in order to "serve the purpose of God" (Acts 13:36).

Chapter 2

THE "WHAT"

Q. What is community analysis?
A. Community analysis, or neighborhood mapping, is a practical approach of learning how to understand and reach your neighborhood in order to effectively proclaim and demonstrate the gospel.

Before we are able to map our neighborhoods, it's important to understand what this process looks like. The Word of God offers some clear direction, as well as a helpful formula designed to take us more deeply into a community.

A LOOK AT SCRIPTURE: HOW PAUL SUCCESSFULLY READ A COMMUNITY

Acts 17:16–31 provides a scriptural framework for community analysis. As you read these verses, note (particularly in the verses I bolded) how the apostle Paul was a culture broker, an astute exegete of culture who understood audiences.

While Paul was waiting for [Silas and Timothy] at Athens, **his spirit was being provoked within him as he was observing the city full of idols.** So he was reasoning in the synagogue with the Jews and the God-fearing Gentiles, and in the market place every day with those who happened to be present. And also some of the Epicurean and Stoic philosophers were conversing with him. Some were saying, "What would this idle babbler wish to say?" Others, "He seems to be a proclaimer of strange deities,"—because he was preaching Jesus and the resurrection. And they took him and brought him to the Areopagus, saying, "May we know what this new teaching is which you are proclaiming? For you are bringing some strange things to our ears; so we want to know what these things mean." (Now all the Athenians and the strangers visiting there used to spend their time in nothing other than telling or hearing something new.)

So Paul stood in the midst of the Areopagus and said, "Men of Athens, **I observe that you are very religious in all respects. For while I was passing through and examining the objects of your worship,** I also found an altar with this inscription, 'TO AN UNKNOWN GOD.' Therefore what you worship in ignorance, this I proclaim to you. The God who made the world and all things in it, since He is Lord of heaven and earth, does not dwell in temples made with hands; nor is He served by human hands, as though He needed anything, since He Himself gives to all people life and breath and all things; and He made from one man every nation of mankind to live on all the face of the earth, having determined their appointed times and the boundaries of their habitation, that they would seek God, if perhaps they might grope for Him and find Him, though He is not far from each one of us; for in Him we live and move and exist, as even some of your own poets have said, 'For we also are His children.' Being then the children of God, we ought not to think that the Divine Nature is like gold or silver or stone, an image formed by the art and thought of man. Therefore having overlooked the times of ignorance, God is now declaring to men that all people everywhere should repent, because He has fixed a day in which He will judge the world in righteousness through a Man whom He has appointed, having furnished proof to all men by raising Him from the dead."

The apostle Paul did three things as he "read" the community in which he found himself.

1. Initial observation. The first thing Paul did while waiting for Silas and Timothy to arrive was to observe, or glance at, his surroundings. My older version of the NASB says that he *beheld*. This was just an initial look, a first glance. He noticed things that needed biblical attention.[1] So much of understanding a community is seeing the need, being willing to be in it, walk in it, experience it. Do we see? Do we allow God to break our hearts over our communities in the tragic disconnect between who Christ is and who the community is?

2. Deeper observation. In verse 22, we read that Paul told the group that he had been taking a closer look, an *observation*. It's about going deeper. He had time to muse and reflect. He was considering how what he'd seen was broken and what God's solution might be. This was a move from the "what" to the "how" of the issue.

3. Examination. He continued in verse 23 by saying he examined the objects of their worship. This word is the deepest of the three, reflecting an analytical process. He was now hypothesizing the "why" of the issue. He worked toward understanding their lifestyle and language, in order to tap into their longings. He moved into an aspect of engaging them relationally and trying to make sense out of this community, to find things in common, which led him to the boldness to proclaim truth to them.

Paul's posture is a model we can follow. He told them, "You're amazing! You are so sincere. You are seeking." He didn't chide them for what they were missing. He affirmed them for the fact that they were seeking. By verse 27, he was able to offer them the biblical solution they'd been looking for.

SO WHAT?

In the early 1990s pastor Leith Anderson put together a helpful formula for what community analysis looks like.[2] He wrote that *diagnosis* (D) plus *prescription* (Rx), along with *hard work* (HW) and the *power of God* (PG) results in a changed community.

(D+Rx) HW + PG = Changed Church/Community

Let's unpack each of those aspects of the formula to help us better understand the strategic way we come to a neighborhood.

Diagnosis (D). I use the vowels *a, e, i, o, u* to help clarify what this means: *analyze, examine, inspect, observe,* and *uncover.* We use all of these techniques in order to discover the community. It implies a rigorous or disciplined pursuit.

Prescription (Rx). Based on that analysis or diagnosis, we prescribe an answer or a strategy, in a sense, a biblical solution. Think of it in medical terms. When we go to a doctor for any health issue, our bodies are checked out and diagnosed—that diagnosis is about getting to the root of what is causing the ailment. From that diagnosis the doctor then prescribes an antidote, a medicine to bring a greater level of healing. In a similar way, as Christ-followers, we look to weave the gospel into the fabric of a community, so we come as ministry practitioners, sort of spiritual doctors.

> SO MUCH OF OUR TRAINING IS IN HOW TO EXEGETE SCRIPTURE, BUT TO COMPLEMENT THAT WE MUST LEARN TO EXEGETE OUR AUDIENCE.

We understand the amount of training and the years of medical study that one goes through in order to properly diagnose a patient. From a ministry standpoint, we need not neglect or take lightly the work of analyzing or inspecting our communities. We do so at a damaging cost.

Many of us were raised in environments that are unlike the places God has called us to. I was raised in a small, predominantly Caucasian, town in Michigan. But God's calling on my life has been in big cities, such as Chicago, Los Angeles, and the San Francisco Bay area, where I lived as a minority in ethnically and culturally diverse areas. I had a lot of learning to do.

So much of our training is in how to exegete Scripture, but to complement that we must learn to exegete our audience. Unwittingly, though, we can come to a neighborhood and misdiagnose, thinking we know the community, that we have a plan, that we're streetwise, and we may miss the bigger picture of what is there culturally and socioeconomically. We may miss opportunities to connect with gate-keepers or insiders who understand and have deep, vested interests and know-how of the community, and who God may want us to partner with. We may end up being guilty of spiritual malpractice! It's difficult to discover the right spiritual antidote or cure that a community needs when we don't do the work of properly diagnosing it.

Too often we haven't truly diagnosed the needs of a community. Instead we give them a Bible bandage ("God loves you and has a wonderful plan for your life"). But one of the greatest gifts we can give is a proper diagnosis. It may be, along with giving a Bible, that we also give a job to someone who needs work. That is the good news! Good news is more than a message; it's a lifestyle. When we properly diagnose the needs, we are on our way to earning the right to speak the gospel into our neighbors' lives.

Hard Work (HW). The reality is that there are no shortcuts, no easy ways to hurry through the process of learning a community. The Bible gives us incentive in our hard work. Galatians 6:9 tells us not to "lose heart in doing good, for in due time we will reap *if we do not grow weary*" (italics added). First Corinthians 15:58 says, "Be steadfast, immovable, always abounding in the work of the Lord, knowing that your toil," or your labor, "is not in vain in the Lord." And Colossians 1:29 says, "For this purpose also I labor, striving according to His power, which mightily works within me."

It's difficult work to analyze and inspect a community, to exegete culture. It's challenging because it's also changing: diversity, socio-economic changes, neighborhoods that flip, gentrification. With all these things, a church or group of people seeking to plant a church can very quickly find themselves on the outside. So it takes work to keep up with the changing nature of our communities. There is a laborious sense of doing this process and working this formula. Of course God gives us joy in the journey. There is no greater delight than being engaged in kingdom activity. But Scripture does remind us that the work of advancing the gospel requires sacrifice, endurance, perseverance, and a willingness to truly give our all until Christ is formed in a culture and community.

Power of God (PG). If God doesn't build the house, the psalmist says (127:1), then we labor in vain. Zechariah 4:6 reminds us, "'Not by might nor by power, but by My Spirit,' says the LORD of hosts." We are coupled together in deep, utter dependency on the power of God to go forward in our work.

You may look at this formula and think, *The power of God should be first.* Yes, it should! It should be at the beginning, the middle, and the end. We are completely dependent on the power of the Holy Spirit. This formula is not meant for us simply to gear up on all our skills and training and analysis and reading the neighborhood and studying the culture and thinking, *Okay, we got this.* Not at all. The reality is God *must* march before us and it is His power that leads us. We work in tandem, following the Holy Spirit.

And this all results in a changed community and changed church.

APPLICATION

This is the mission of the church:

1. We do an initial look at the community.
2. We allow our spirits to be provoked. We allow God's Spirit to break our hearts for the people in our neighborhood.
3. We observe more deeply.
4. We examine the community. We see the need and form a diagnosis.
5. We do the hard work of responding to the need and engaging the audience.

6. We offer the spiritual antidote to the community's needs.

7. We rely totally and completely on the power of God's Spirit to lead us.

The reality is that this type of work needs to be lived out over a multiyear, multifaceted project. It will take commitment, sacrifice, and a willingness to stay-the-course to what the community needs. And then continuing working through that analysis and formula consistently as the community continues to change and evolve.

CASE STUDY: MOBILIZING OUR YOUTH

When I began to study our small city of 20,000, I had no idea how deeply it would influence the culture of the surrounding neighborhoods. What started as a graduate school project ended up shaping the ministry of a church over the next five years.

As I developed our church's plan to explore the felt needs of the neighborhoods surrounding us, I was excited to see the Lord open doors I never thought possible. In March 2008 our city's (non-Christian) mayor asked me to create a task force specifically focused on addressing the issues in the very neighborhoods we wanted to study. This unsolicited call led to a partnership with local pastors, business leaders, civic leaders, and residents, which allowed us to have a loud voice for change in our community. With the backing of this group, known as the HOPE (Healthy choices, Ownership, Pride, and Excellence) task force, along with funding from a Christian grant foundation and the city government, we developed and eventually a strategic plan to address the spiritual, emotional, physical, and safety needs of the people in our community.

One of the greatest blessings for the church and our city was that we used students from our local churches to canvass the neighborhoods to gather the information. Doing so, we modeled that students are present-day contributors to our city and more importantly to our churches. They are not merely a resource for the future but rather an untapped gold mine for change today! These amazing students knocked on more than 2,100 doors over the next six months and conducted a survey that gathered information on family composition, economic status, safety concerns, government assistance utilized, and church affiliation or spiritual leanings. We then used this information to develop ministry that helped reach spiritual and physical needs, while the city used it to develop a strategic plan to help foster quality of life in these neighborhoods. Best of all it led to several direct partnerships between the local church and local government to meet these needs together. During Hurricane Irene and other natural disasters, the partnerships forged during this process have helped strengthen our city's and church's response.

As of 2013 these partnerships continue to grow. In the past year our church has helped the city obtain grants for youth drug prevention and for a new park for children. The city is a better place to live because the church stepped up and mobilized in partnership with the city.

ROB TOWNSHEND
Youth Pastor, Lake Sawyer Christian Church
Black Diamond, Washington

Chapter 3

THE "WHY"

Q. *Why perform community analysis?*
A. *Because community analysis—knowing who the people are and their specific needs—is God's heart.*

The prophet Jeremiah tells us to "seek the welfare of the city where I have sent you . . . and pray to the LORD on its behalf; for in its welfare you will have welfare." An older version of the NASB says to seek the shalom, or peace, of the city. Why do we engage in community analysis? The simple answer is so that we may bring about peace, harmony, welfare, and fullness to those around us. Because that is what God calls us to do. He calls us to pray on our neighborhoods' behalf. But not only to seek shalom for our neighbors, we also discover God's heart through prayer.

Therefore, community analysis must begin with prayer. We must first get to know the community through God's eyes. Sheryl Montgomery Wingerd, a missionary with South Asia Now, reminds us that in order to successfully reach our neighbors, God's people are to be "studying their city, taking responsibility to know its strengths and weaknesses, its needs and possibilities.... [We are to be] the ones walking the perimeter, standing on its corners, interacting with life on the streets, absorbing the atmosphere ... making the effort on behalf of neighbors who cannot cry out for themselves."[1] Rather than creating more programs and events that move us toward busyness or meeting our own needs, we wait on the Lord to give us a love for the community and its people.

> **WHEN WE SEEK THE COMMUNITY'S WELFARE AND THEY ENJOY PEACE AND WELLNESS AND JOY, THEN OUR REWARD IS THAT WE DO TOO!**

Going back to Acts 17, which we discussed earlier, we see that Paul's spirit "was being provoked" (v. 16). Our spirits must be stirred to be truly engaged in our communities. Only then can God's hand work through us.

But there's another reason for engaging in community analysis. The second part of Jeremiah 29:7 tells us: "In its welfare you will have welfare." In other words, when we seek the community's welfare and they enjoy peace and wellness and joy, then our reward is that we do too!

A LOOK AT SCRIPTURE: ESTHER 4:13–17

Then Mordecai told them to reply to Esther, "Do not imagine that you in the king's palace can escape any more than all the Jews. For if you remain silent at this time, relief and deliverance will arise for the Jews from another place and you and your father's house will perish. And who knows whether you have not attained royalty for such a time as this?"

Then Esther told them to reply to Mordecai, "Go, assemble all the Jews who are found in Susa, and fast for me; do not eat or drink for three days, night or day. I and my maidens also will fast in the same way. And thus I will go in to the king, which is not according to the law; and if I perish, I perish." So Mordecai went away and did just as Esther had commanded him.

This passage points to the significance of an "Esther moment." By that I mean, the opportunity to respond in an urgent and pertinent way to the needs of our community. In fact, this Scripture reminds us that we too have "come into the kingdom" for "such a time as this." Esther models for us a pattern that spells out why we should respond to the needs of our day.

1. *Context*: The sovereignty of God had strategically placed Esther as a person of influence within her culture. This book states nine times that she had been given favor by God. Even though she was up against formidable odds, she understood the need to act on behalf of her people. Despite differing circumstances, God has placed us in a position to respond to the needs around us. We too have been given favor by God (such as access to resources and people of influence whom we can recruit to join us in the work). It is up to us to act accordingly.

2. *Compassion*: Earlier in chapter 4 Esther heard the news about Haman's despicable plot to "destroy, to kill and to annihilate all the Jews" (3:13). It was not enough just to put them to death, but the intent was to utterly wipe them out. Her response was deeply convicting; she "writhed in great anguish" (4:4), so much so that she could not endure the horrors that were about to befall her people (8:6). Esther responded with God's heart of compassion for her people. Have we reached this same point of desperation around the plight of our communities? Until we do, is it any wonder that we do not see deep change in our neighborhoods? God, give us tears and move us to action.

3. *Consecration*: Before Esther jumped into action, she paused to fast for several days. She dedicated her life to be used for God's purposes. As we anticipate serving in our communities, before we rush headlong into the needs, we must ensure that our hearts and minds are at God's disposal.

4. *Courage*: Esther counted the cost and was willing to give her life for the sake of her people. Her words to Mordecai were, "If I perish, I

perish." There is risk in engaging broken places: sacrificing time with family, being misunderstood by friends, safety concerns . . . and we will need courage like Esther had to remain faithful to our calling.

5. *Commitment*: Esther could not remain silent in the broken state of her people (7:4). She responded by speaking on their behalf to the king, risking her own reputation by doing so. Her commitment to act was rewarded by the king sparing her people, and the fear of God was instilled into the community (9:1–4). Actions lead to results. Imagine what God can do in your community through your commitment and dedication.

So What?

Read and meditate on Psalm 122:6–8.

Pray for the peace of Jerusalem:
"May they prosper who love you.
May peace be within your walls,
And prosperity within your palaces."
For the sake of my brothers and my friends,
I will now say, "May peace be within you."

This psalm contains a "Prayer for the Community," drawn from Robert Linthicum's *City of God, City of Satan*.[2] It's a model of how to pray for the neighborhood broken into five parts.

1. *Spiritual vitality* (v. 6a). The first thing we ask God for is our community to abound in spiritual vitality: "Pray for the peace of Jerusalem." Or "Pray for the peace of Uptown," or "Pray for the peace of Lakeview." We pray for God to give our neighborhood peace, shalom.

2. *Economic health* (v. 6b). Next we ask God to allow the area to thrive through economic health: "May they prosper who love you." When an area prospers, it receives resources it otherwise cannot receive. That in turn allows the area to better flourish.

3. *Physical safety* (v. 7a). There are a lot of neighborhoods where physical safety is a luxury. Every day we can tune into the news and hear or read about another shooting, robbery, mugging, or some other violence that is happening. Even the best neighborhoods can have violence. So we ask God to provide physical safety to our neighbors: "May peace be within your walls."

4. *Political justice* (v. 7b). Our communities need justice. They desperately need fair opportunities. And so we pray for God to bring "prosperity within your palaces."

5. *Social relationships* (v. 8). Throughout the prayer we've asked God to provide peace and prosperity to "the land," so to speak. This final request is to ask God to bring peace to each person in the community: "For the sake of my brothers and my friends, I will now say, 'May peace be within you.'" This is where God softens the hearts of our neighbors and allows them to be open to the gospel.

Haddon Anderson, a youth pastor and former student of mine, recently told me about a man his church had ministered to by helping him find employment. The man was so excited to have work. Haddon said, "He's now been employed for two months and when I saw him the other day, he told me how happy he was that he gets to do something meaningful and support his family." The church became relevant in that man's—and family's—life. Deep in the human heart, there is the desire to be able to maintain and provide, and the church offered that opportunity to Haddon's new friend. This is just one story of thousands that when we hear them, we are able to connect God's story, and in the process of that, you can connect your own story. It all weaves together.

APPLICATION

One of the best ways to discover why community analysis is important is to first observe the area (as Paul did in Acts 17), and then pray over the area. Before we survey or interview or do any other work, we pray. And what better way to pray and get to observe a community than to initiate prayer-walking. Prayer-walking is simply praying as we walk, but focused on a specific locale. It is praying on-site, with insight. It's an unobtrusive, effective way to place ourselves before God and intercede for people and places. In a physical sense, we draw nearer to pray clearer.

An example of a type of prayer-walking is what the Israelites did around Jericho.

> Now Jericho was tightly shut . . . [But] the LORD said to Joshua, "See, I have given Jericho into your hand, with its king *and* the valiant warriors. You shall march around the city. . . . When you hear the sound of the trumpet, all the people shall shout with a great shout; and the wall of the city will fall down flat." (Josh. 6:1–5)

As the walls of Jericho crumbled and collapsed because the Israelites honored God, so too we believe that spiritual walls in our neighborhoods can begin to come down as a result of the concentrated prayers of God's people. As we walk and pray over our communities, we get a sense of the personal helplessness of those around us, we see how the place itself impacts the people, and our faith is stretched. Cofounder of the Salvation Army, Catherine Booth, once said, "Oh that we could weep the gospel into people." Prayer-walking helps build our understanding, grows our spiritual authority, and drives us to the compassion that brings about weeping the gospel into people.

I have found it helpful to base our prayer-walking efforts on a strong biblical theology, following in the footsteps, so to speak, of countless other believers who have cried out to God for their communities as well. God has tugged on my own heart, and so many others, as we have prayer-walked our way through numerous neighborhoods of Chicago the past two decades. It is my sincere desire that the following practical steps on where and how to pray-walk will encourage you in your prayer-walking endeavors as it has for me.

STEPS TO PRAYER-WALKING

1. *Identify the neighborhood.* Purchase a map of your city or neighborhood. Then identify streets, neighborhoods, and key areas central to its spiritual and social well-being, including significant people living and working in your community. I had the privilege of completing the Chicago Neighborhood Prayer Guide in partnership with several other ministries and churches in order to mobilize people to pray for all seventy-seven neighborhoods in Chicago. Our goal was to recognize key social and spiritual prayer concerns and unique characters of each of these communities, which churches and ministries could then use as a model for other cities to use as well.[3]

2. *Invite others to join you.* Research which people and organizations you want to invite to come along and those you want to visit on your prayer-walk. Both are important. A great way to build unity among believers is to get other like-minded Christians in the area to pray as well. This isn't about building up a specific church; this is about reaching people for the kingdom and about glorifying God's name. So share this opportunity with neighboring partner churches and make announcements leading up to the prayer-walk.

On the walk you'll also want to stop by specific places to pray for them. For instance, I was recently part of my church's prayer-walking group, which covered a Chicago neighborhood that used to be identified with the Cabrini Green housing projects. We walked the streets and prayed, but we also went into apartment complexes and prayed in the halls.

3. *Map out your route and set a date for the prayer-walk.* Be clear about the perimeters of your walk and share that with all who will join you. Make copies of the neighborhood map so that everyone knows where to go.

4. *Prep your neighbors.* Let area schools, homes, businesses know you're planning to pray for them and when. That way they know what you're doing, see you taking an active interest in the community, and

it will provide opportunities for them to approach you for prayer or with questions.

5. Put people into teams. You don't want an oversized group walking the streets. Send your people out in pairs or trios, so that the entire neighborhood is covered all at once.

6. Set a time frame. This doesn't need to be an all-day event. Limit it to one to two hours. Also, encourage the teams to rotate and change routes throughout the time frame.

7. Be discreet. It's important to avoid pretense or showiness. You're quietly in the neighborhood, yet walking through the streets, taking them for God.

8. Pray as specifically as you can. Pray for spiritual breakthroughs, souls, families, peace, safety, vocational, and education needs, as well as any other needs you know of.

9. Pause at strategic places. Be silent and wait on God to speak. Listen to the activities around you. Listen for the Holy Spirit's voice.

10. Offer praise as well as prayer. Sing songs of praise as you move through the neighborhood. You might sing "God of This City," or "Amazing Grace." Something that keeps you focused on how great our God is and what He desires to do in this community—through you.

Remember that the book of James tells us that "the effective prayer of a righteous man can accomplish much" (5:16). Never underestimate the power of prayer-walking. As you continue to cover your neighborhood with prayer, you may decide to creatively switch it up. On the far South Side of Chicago in the Roseland neighborhood, Pastor James Meeks and his congregation at Salem Baptist Church recently set up prayer corners where they have unleashed hundreds of their congregants to engage the broader community in prayer and gospel conversation. They have seen hundreds of people come to Jesus as a result of their obedience.

If you still need a bit more convincing on why community analysis is so important, let the words of this modern hymn settle into your soul:

> *Our cities cry to You, O God, from out of their pain and strife; You made us for Yourself alone, but we choose alien life. Our goals are pleasure, gold, and power; injustice stalks our earth; in vain we seek for rest, for joy, for sense of human worth.*
>
> *Yet still You walk our street, O Christ! We know Your presence here where humble Christians love and serve in godly grace and fear. O Word made flesh, be seen in us! May all we say and do affirm You God, Incarnate still, and turn sad hearts to You!*
>
> *Your people are Your hands and feet to serve Your world today, our lives the book our cities read to help them find Your way. O pour Your sovereign Spirit out on heart and will and brain; inspire Your Church with love and power to ease our cities' pain!*
>
> *O Healing Savior, Prince of Peace, salvation's Source and Sum, for You our broken cities cry—O come, Lord Jesus, Come! With truth, Your royal diadem, with righteousness Your rod, O Come, Lord Jesus, bring to earth the City of our God! Amen.*[4]

CASE STUDY: PARTNERING WITH A LOCAL SCHOOL

I had the pleasure of meeting Doc Fuder at Moody's Pastors' Conference in 2005. Our new church was only three weeks old and I was excited to learn all I could about urban ministry. I was the first one in the classroom that Tuesday morning. I arrived early to get a good seat. When Doc began to teach us hungry men about God's heart for the poor and marginalized, I felt my own heart begin to weep as well. As he continued to teach us, he shared how important community analysis is for our churches. This was the first concept of community analysis I'd ever heard. I left that conference and took my new knowledge back home with me. Since then, our church has adopted this methodology of outreach and evangelism, and we've touched our community in many special ways.

The first thing we did was to pray for God to break our hearts for the community. He did. We then began to pay close attention to the needs and happenings in the various areas. Rock Island is very diverse and composed of several neighborhoods that are divided by names. We began to walk those areas and pray over them. As we walked, we cleaned up garbage and litter on those streets. God quickly opened the doors of ministry as we watched and learned.

Early one chilly morning in 2008, I received a phone call from the police department. Our church, which is across from a middle school, had been vandalized by one of the students. Our youth director and I responded immediately. The police and the principal asked if we wanted to press charges and have the boy arrested. We declined and were able to minister to this boy and his broken family. We then began to sponsor a program at the school that awards students who improve their behavior, grades, and attendance every quarter. Since then, our youth director and his family also moved into the neighborhood. He now helps coach the junior football teams.

We have also recently opened a community center next door to the church. And we will soon provide preschool screenings, medical exams, legal advice, and financial guidance as well as English lessons for our growing African population.

Thank you, Doc Fuder, for pouring so much of your God-given passion into all of us. Community analysis has completely changed the way we do ministry.

TOM SCHILLINGER
Pastor, Mighty Fortress Community Church
Rock Island, Illinois

Chapter 4

THE "WHO"

Q. *Who performs community analysis?*

A. *Community analysis is made effective by those whose hearts have been broken with compassion and who desire to share the good news of Christ.*

Not everyone in our churches is going to clearly connect with the call to go out into the fields and reap the harvest. That's why we start our mission with prayer. Because as we discussed in the previous "why" section, we pray for God to break our hearts, to make us feel deeply the pains and longings of those physically surrounding our churches.

Compassion does not happen overnight, in the classroom, or even in church. In fact, this work of the heart takes months and years to cultivate and is learned on the streets. My friend Jonathan Nambu, who founded and serves with Samaritana in Manila, once told me, "In order to be for a community, you must first be with a community." Compassion doesn't come from afar; it's nurtured and grown when it's with those people who most desperately need it. Jesus is the perfect example: He came to earth to *live among us* (John 1:14). The meaning of compassion comes from the Latin "to suffer with." Jesus suffered with us. When we cultivate compassion, we have chosen to come alongside those who are suffering and identify with them.

The late theologian and author Henri Nouwen, in his outstanding work simply titled *Compassion*, defined the concept for us:

> The word *compassion* is derived from the Latin words *pati* and *cum*, which together mean "to suffer with." Compassion asks us to go where it hurts, to enter into places of pain, to share in brokenness, fear, confusion, anguish. Compassion challenges us to cry out with those in misery, to mourn with those who are lonely, to weep with those in tears. Compassion requires us to be weak with the weak, vulnerable with the vulnerable, and powerless with the powerless. Compassion means full immersion with the condition of being human.[1]

Nouwen built on the same theme in *The Return of the Prodigal Son*:

> Perhaps the most radical statement Jesus ever made is: "Be compassionate even as your Father is compassionate" (Luke 6:36). He invites me to become like God and show the same compassion to others He is showing to me. Jesus wants to make it clear that God is a God of compassion. If God is compassionate, then certainly those who love God should be compassionate as well. This is the core message of the gospel. We are called to love with absolute compassion.[2]

It is important to know that people in the community do not need sympathy or pity, but they are open to genuine friendship. Community analysis does not come to monopolize the work being done in an area. We should instead come to serve the body of Christ and learn from those who have already been there before us. Also, we do not come to be caretakers but rather empowerers. We come alongside, as coaches or leaders, allowing and encouraging our neighbors with dignity. As we seek to understand the community, it will be important to examine our hearts and repent of any superiority or paternalistic attitudes.

Only when we are broken can we truly minister to others. Our authority is found in our compassion, in our brokenness. Too often we want to blame the neighborhood for our issues and prejudices. Only then have we earned the right to speak into someone's pain, and only then do we have the ability and opportunity to become an insider in the community.

A LOOK AT SCRIPTURE: BECOMING AN INSIDER

An insider is a person who has won the trust of the community and learned how to build relationships in the area. Becoming an insider involves a willingness to be a learner, to be instructed and informed by knowledgeable individuals who can swing open the doors to a particular subculture. It requires consistent, visible presence in a community of need. In major cities, the needs of those on the street vary minimally yet persist consistently. We are in short supply of consecrated, compassionate men and women who are willing to become insiders in order to penetrate such cultures and people groups in our communities. Here are several biblical principles to help prepare you to be an insider in your community.

> WE DON'T NEED TO REINVENT THE MINISTRY WHEEL. WE CAN FIND THOSE WHO HAVE BEEN WORKING IN THE COMMUNITY AND WHO KNOW THE CULTURE THERE AND PARTNER WITH THEM.

1. God is already at work in the community.

"[Jesus] answered them, 'My Father is working until now, and I Myself am working'" (John 5:17).

God has already been at work in the community for a long time, particularly in broken neighborhoods. So in many respects we don't need to reinvent the ministry wheel. We can find those who have been working in the community and who know the culture there and partner with them. Take time to visit God's people in churches and ministries who live and work in the community. Reach out and seek the advice and counsel of those who have spent years getting to know their neighbors. Visit the local law enforcement, social workers, schoolteachers, businesses, public officials, and others who live in the community, not just Christians, to see how you can integrate your efforts with those who have a genuine concern for the community. As you meet various people, look for the "man of peace" (Luke 10), an informant or gatekeeper or culture broker who understands the community's history and has access into its culture and life.

When my wife and I moved to East San Jose in the early 1980s with City Team Ministries, we met a Christ-follower, Connie, who lived in the Meadowfair neighborhood. We were the only white couple in the community and we befriended this dear Latina woman who had multiple relationships throughout the area. She became a gatekeeper for us. Through her and others, we were able to start Bible studies and ultimately see a church planted. We couldn't have accomplished all that we did without Connie—and her presence there reminded us that God was at work long before we even showed up.

2. Remember that you are a weak vessel.

"[God] has said to me, 'My grace is sufficient for you, for power is perfected in weakness.' Most gladly, therefore, I will rather boast about my weaknesses, so that the power of Christ may dwell in me" (2 Cor. 12:9).

The apostle Paul reminded us that we do *all* things through Christ who gives us strength. One of the more humbling experiences is to go into a community and exegete it, read it, learn it. It is amazing how little we know about a culture, ethnic group, or place, even though we may have lived there for years. If we go into our neighborhoods on our own strength and "wisdom," we will lose the battle. And it is a battle—a long, hard fight to win souls for Christ. But thank God, we do not fight alone.

We go in our weakness, not in our strength. That is crucial to learning how to exegete a community. There are people there who can teach us. When we go in our weakness, by asking, "Would you help me understand?" we see God's strength at work.

3. Bathe everything you do in prayer.

"Confess your sins to one another, and pray for one another so that you may be healed. The effective prayer of a righteous man can accomplish much" (James 5:16).

"Seek the welfare of the city where I have sent you into exile, and pray to the LORD on its behalf; for in its welfare you will have welfare" (Jer. 29:7).

We've talked extensively about the power and importance of prayer, but it deserves to be repeated. We need to depend completely on God and His leading. That means continuous reaching out to God for wisdom, strength, discernment, power, miracles, and blessing.

4. Step out in obedience and persist faithfully.

"Be steadfast, immovable, always abounding in the work of the Lord, knowing that your toil is not in vain in the Lord" (1 Cor. 15:58).

"I will most gladly spend and be expended for your souls. If I love you more, am I to be loved less?" (2 Cor. 12:15).

We know that God's heart is for the people in our communities—those not only inside the church but outside its walls. It's a long process to reach those in need. Because of that, we need to take seriously the commitment God has called us to. When we go obediently, we become willing to let our hearts be broken for the people God has called us to reach. In the darkest times, in the most frustrating times, we stay true to the call, knowing that the one who called us to the task is faithful. Henri Nouwen wrote in *The Wounded Healer* that ultimately when God's people take on the wounds of the world, then we ultimately understand what it means to be followers of Christ.

5. Go as a learner and be vulnerable.

"The Word became flesh, and dwelt among us, and we saw His glory, glory as of the only begotten from the Father, full of grace and truth" (John 1:14).

"Have this attitude in yourselves which was also in Christ Jesus, who, although He existed in the form of God, did not regard equality with God a thing to be grasped, but emptied Himself, taking the form of a bond-servant, *and* being made in the likeness of men. Being found in appearance as a man, He humbled Himself by becoming obedient to the point of death, even death on a cross" (Phil. 2:5–8).

The people we meet have a lot to teach us before we can share the gospel with them. Too often we go into a community with an agenda instead of asking questions to discover who these people are we are trying to reach. When we go to the streets as a learner, and are willing to be vulnerable, we give dignity to the people we are learning from. By listening, we give value to them.

Let's break down the Philippians passage to better understand the four ways in which God wants us to present ourselves to our communities.[3]

He wants us to go from pride to humility. Verse 5 says that we are to "have this attitude in [ourselves] which was also in Christ Jesus."

He wants us to go from harmony to dysfunction. That doesn't sound so great, does it? But consider verse 6: Christ, "who, although He existed in the form of God, did not regard equality with God a thing to be grasped." In other words God emptied Himself and entered our chaos and mess. The world is a broken place and God desires for us to push into the mess and live among it, in order to bring peace.

He wants us to go from privilege to poverty. Many of our neighborhoods are impoverished. We are a privileged people who have access to resources. We can choose to remove our children from the "bad" schools to enroll them in better, safer schools, for instance. But many people can't. God calls us to set aside our privilege and truly reside among those who have nothing, following Christ's model in verse 7: "[Jesus] emptied Himself, taking the form of a bond-servant, and being made in the likeness of men."

He wants us to go from power to powerlessness. This is a difficult one because the real struggles in our lives often come down to power versus powerlessness. Yet according to verse 8, we know that Jesus "being found in appearance as a man . . . humbled Himself by becoming obedient to the point of death, even death on a cross."

6. God keeps those whom He calls as insiders.

"Have I not commanded you? Be strong and courageous! Do not tremble or be dismayed, for the LORD your God is with you wherever you go" (Josh. 1:9).

"I love You, O LORD, my strength."
The LORD is my rock and my fortress and my deliverer,
My God, my rock, in whom I take refuge;
My shield and the horn of my salvation, my stronghold.
I call upon the LORD, who is worthy to be praised,
And I am saved from my enemies." (Ps. 18:1–3)

What a beautiful reminder we have from these two passages: God will not leave us to do the work alone. He is faithful and He goes ahead of us to lead the way for us. We can trust that God will sustain as He directs.

7. We must revisit "doing church" on the streets.

"The head of the household . . . said to his slave, 'Go out at once into the streets and lanes of the city and bring in here the poor and crippled and blind and lame.' And the slave said, 'Master, what you commanded has been done, and still there is room.' And the master said to the slave, 'Go out into the highways and along the hedges, and compel them to come in, so that my house may be filled'" (Luke 14:21–23).

For too long the church has worked under the impression that people in need should come into the building to receive help, comfort, and compassion. But that's not what Jesus taught. We are to go out and get them. We don't wait for them to come to us; we go to them. We love them in such a way that we *compel* them to come to faith.

Plead, persuade, and beg. Isn't it fascinating that the mandate is to go out to the broken, to the hurting, to the weak. Weep with them so that God's house will truly be known as a place for *all* people. I firmly believe that analyzing a community gives us the tools to be able to that.

8. Compassion is at the core of our commitment.

"Go and learn what this means: 'I DESIRE COMPASSION, AND NOT SACRIFICE,' for I did not come to call the righteous, but sinners.... Seeing the people, He felt compassion for them, because they were distressed and dispirited like sheep without a shepherd" (Matt. 9:13, 36).

> WE DON'T JUST ARRIVE AT COMPASSION; WE GROW IT OVER TIME AND EXPERIENCES.

"When Jesus went ashore, He saw a large crowd, and He felt compassion for them because they were like sheep without a shepherd; and He began to teach them many things" (Mark 6:34).

Sometimes we may feel overconfident and overcompetent. *Oh, it's not a big deal,* we think. *I know this neighborhood. I've been here before. We can do this; we just need to preach the gospel and people will change.* But I think the harder, gut-level honest point is that we may have to face prejudice, which is deeper in us than we may realize. Any of us who were raised in a monocultural environment, for instance, won't fully understand the depth of what prejudice really looks like, to prejudge another person, or presume a certain amount of favor over another culture—whether it's ethnically or socioeconomically—runs deep. Professor and author Dr. David Augsburger has said, "He who knows but one culture knows no culture."

Also, a lot of times we may feel guilty that we haven't done more in the community. We've run, we've moved, we've sheltered ourselves away, and stayed comfortably inside the walls of the church. We know little about our city, neighborhood, suburb. Only those who truly have a heart of compassion are able to effectively engage in community analysis—and this is a lifelong commitment. We don't just arrive at compassion; we grow it over time and experiences. In many respects as God begins to work with us, we will begin to feel overwhelmed and vulnerable—and that's a good thing! The more compassionate you become, the more you may feel the weight of the world. The key is what we do with that feeling. At times you may feel anxious or worried with the revelation of, "God, this is bigger than us!" Yet in that feeling of spiritual hurt is also spiritual anger: "Oh, God, forgive me. I want to become more aware, more intuned to Your people. I haven't wept over Your communities. I haven't cared about the darkest places where they need You so much. But God, I commit anew to go where You lead." In our inadequacy, our brokenness, we come to a place of confession and commitment. That's when real compassion grows.

When I was doing my doctoral work, for my dissertation, I put together a "compassion continuum" to help us gage and reflect on where we are.

"The Compassion Continuum"[4]

STAGE 1 Pre-exposure	STAGE 2 "Seeing"	STAGE 3 "Feeling"			STAGE 4 "Acting"
+ Enthusiasm		LEVEL 1	TRANSITION	LEVEL 2*	COMPASSION "TO SUFFER WITH"
+ Teachability	EXPOSURE TO URBAN NEED	Vulnerable	Discouraged	Acceptance	Incarnation
+Naïveté		Intimidated	Frustrated	Confession	Identification
o Indifference		Overwhelmed	Disillusioned	Commitment	Empowerment
- Overconfidence		Anxious	Helpless	Conviction	Servanthood
- Prejudice		Hurt	Inadequate		Brokenness
- Fear		Angry			
- Guilt					

KEY:

+ Positive   o Neutral   - Negative

*Denotes a cyclical pattern

We all start at Stage 1, that oblivious, safe place of pre-exposure, in which we live sheltered, unaware of the needs of people unlike us.

Then something happens that pushes us into Stage 2, in which we are exposed to an unfamiliar, uncomfortable place. We see the desperation of people's lives and circumstances. As our eyes are opened to those around us, we enter the "feeling" stage, or Stage 3. This stage includes a progression where we first deal with the uncontrollable issues. We may have righteous anger but aren't sure how to handle the situation; or we feel overwhelmed by the sheer amount of need. That eventually moves us into a transitional period in which we feel disillusioned, helpless, inadequate, and frustrated. The important thing to remember when you're in this transitional period is that God has you exactly where He wants you. You are at the gateway to compassion. As you press ahead, you eventually move into the next level of Stage 3, which is the place of acceptance. You are moved to commitment and an unfailing conviction. (It's important to note that Stage 3 is a cyclical stage, in which, depending on the circumstances, season of ministry, or a number of other factors, you may find yourself moving back and forth between the levels.)

Finally, with that commitment, you move into Stage 4, which is the "acting" stage. This is where true compassion lies. You identify with the powerless and broken. You seek to empower and serve those around you. You commit to be engaged with those in your world—the poor, the broken, the ethnically and socioeconomically diverse.

Our convictions always come out of our commitments. We are committed to our values, and our convictions will flow out of our commitments.

So where do you find yourself on this continuum?

SO WHAT?

When we realign biblical values with God's heart for these people and this place, out of that we can go to our deacons and denominations and church boards and pound our fists and say, "We must be about the work of this town/community." We must take the light to the darkness—that's what it was made for. We must be salty. Salt is a preservative to keep meat from rotting. Too often the salt is in places where there is no rotten meat and the light is in places where there's already light. That is what compassion is: we suffer with. It's always incarnational; it identifies and walks alongside of the broken.

As we consider the "who" is called to community analysis, it's easy to know that *we* are called.

After all, you've picked up this book, so you're already invested and interested in the subject. But the real question becomes, in what way are we called? And who does God call us *to be* in the midst of His leading?

APPLICATION

As you prepare to engage in community analysis, it's beneficial to ask yourself and your team these questions:

- What does it mean that God is already at work in even the darkest areas? Do I really believe that? In what ways have we missed seeing His handiwork by avoiding these places? What are my fears and concerns?

- What examples of "insiders" are there in the Scriptures? In what ways did God use them to enable His people to accomplish His purposes? What can I learn from those biblical figures, such as Joseph, Esther, Nehemiah, Daniel, Paul?

- What nearby subcultures or community of need could God use me to penetrate with the gospel? Who is an already-established "insider" or culture broker who could let me into that area? What practical steps can I take to make contact?

- How would I assess the state of my heart around the biblical pattern of compassion? If I were to evaluate myself on "learning compassion," what grade would I give myself?

CASE STUDY: MULTIETHNIC COMMUNITY CHURCH PLANT

Planting a church is difficult enough, but I can't imagine trying to do it without a good grasp on the community that I'm planting in. Before setting out on our journey, I instinctively knew that I needed to get a handle on who was in our community, what they believed, valued, and needed, especially in a neighborhood of 64,000 people speaking more than eighty different languages! But instinctively knowing it and knowing how to go about it are often two different things. It was through the principles of community analysis with John Fuder that working this out began to take shape.

After months of prayer, in 2001 my wife and I moved to Chicago's Rogers Park neighborhood on the far North Side of the city. We began wading through the latest census data on our community, meeting with and interviewing community leaders and longtime residents, and conducting a research project based on a survey of a cross section of the neighborhood residents. All this allowed us to put together a comprehensive picture of life in the community and catapulted us from new residents of the neighborhood to insiders because we went in with the attitude of a learner and simply listened to people's stories.

Listening to these stories and hearing about the real and perceived issues gave us a starting place for relationship building. It also helped us focus our energies, outreach, and limited resources, and use them to unlock the hearts of the people with whom we were seeking to share Christ. Even before the church held its first public worship service, the attitude of being a student of the community—an integral part of community analysis—began to pay dividends. Several key influencers began to seek us out for input and perspective, and the local business community development association even asked for permission to use some of our research to help develop a new strategic plan.

In the early life of our church we also had the opportunity to teach some community analysis principles to the people who attended the church. Helping them to be question-askers and observers of life in the neighborhood helped our people move from seeing the neighborhood as more than just the place where they happened to live, to being "their neighborhood," a place where they could invest themselves for the sake of the gospel.

In the years since moving to that neighborhood and planting a church there, we've also taken community analysis into a midsized Midwestern town where we have been involved in restarting a church, and are preparing to go through the process again in a neighboring community as we launch a new work there. The environment may look different, the process may need tweaking, but the principles of community analysis work whether you deal with a monocultural setting or a multicultural one.

DR. TIM BEAVIS
Founding Pastor, Rogers Park Community Church
Chicago, Illinois
Senior Pastor, The Orchard Church
McHenry, Illinois

Chapter 5

THE "WHERE"

Q. Where do we do community analysis?
A. Where God has placed you and your church/ministry.

Dr. Ray Bakke suggests a "theology of place,"[1] that God has not only called people, but He uses specific places as the setting for His purposes to be actualized. As the world globalizes and urbanizes, God uses this strategically in order to advance the gospel to the ends of the earth.

Get to know your community thoroughly. Research the history, patterns of migration, as well as demographic makeup—in short, do all you can to familiarize yourself with the community of your calling and residence. When it comes to place, community analysis is best achieved by those who have made the long-term commitment to stay where they have been called. Many neighborhood residents have seen churches and ministries come and go, unwilling to invest in their communities.

> WHEN IT COMES TO PLACE, COMMUNITY ANALYSIS IS BEST ACHIEVED BY THOSE WHO HAVE MADE THE LONG-TERM COMMITMENT TO STAY WHERE THEY HAVE BEEN CALLED.

Yet it is important to understand that it takes years to show that we are committed to the welfare of the community.

Discern the felt needs of the community, such as crime, unemployment, homelessness, as well as family size, educational attainment, and housing patterns. One suggestion is to ask those you have built relationships with who are already working in the community what they think the five greatest areas of felt need are.

Ask yourself what things the people of the community, Christian and non-Christian, resent that have been done in the name of Christianity and what they may be more open to. What are the cultural forces at work? How do they perceive Christianity? What has God used in the past to bless the community?

A LOOK AT SCRIPTURE: NEHEMIAH

Our communities are full of broken places, which is where we should be engaged. Nehemiah models for us a process for entering those neglected areas and mobilizing a team of people to restore hope and dignity to a marginalized community.

1. See the context: broken people and broken places (Neh. 1:1–3)

> Now it happened in the month Chislev, in the twentieth year, while I [Nehemiah] was in Susa the capitol, that Hanani, one of my brothers, and some men from Judah came; and I asked them concerning the Jews who had escaped and had survived the captivity, and about Jerusalem. They said to me, "The remnant there in the province who survived the captivity are in great distress and reproach, and the wall of Jerusalem is broken down and its gates are burned with fire."

Nehemiah heard about distressed people—the remnant—and a distressed wall. Both were broken. Nehemiah cared not just about the people but also about the place. Many people live in throwaway neighborhoods. Our hearts are broken for the people but we couldn't care less about where they live. Both are important to God.

Our lives are deeply impacted by the places we live. Nehemiah's burden was inflamed by the needs of those who were in Jerusalem, but also by walls that were broken down. It's a graphic image, which we as Christ-followers can understand. Our cities have walls that are crumbling, graffiti-scarred places, and hellish environments that challenge God's people, that call us out to respond with compassion.

2. *Intercede for God's heart* (1:4–11)

When I heard these words, I sat down and wept and mourned for days; and I was fasting and praying before the God of heaven. I said, "I beseech You, O LORD God of heaven, the great and awesome God, who preserves the covenant and lovingkindness for those who love Him and keep His commandments, let Your ear now be attentive and Your eyes open to hear the prayer of Your servant which I am praying before You now, day and night, on behalf of the sons of Israel Your servants, confessing the sins of the sons of Israel which we have sinned against You; I and my father's house have sinned. We have acted very corruptly against You and have not kept the commandments, nor the statutes, nor the ordinances which You commanded Your servant Moses. Remember the word which You commanded Your servant Moses, saying, 'If you are unfaithful I will scatter you among the peoples; but if you return to Me and keep My commandments and do them, though those of you who have been scattered were in the most remote part of the heavens, I will gather them from there and will bring them to the place where I have chosen to cause My name to dwell.' . . . O Lord, I beseech You, may Your ear be attentive to the prayer of Your servant and the prayer of Your servants who delight to revere Your name, and make Your servant successful today and grant him compassion before this man."

When Nehemiah heard the report about Jerusalem, he interceded on their behalf. Rather than try to rush in to fix it, he prayed with tears for many days. Has God given you tears for your city? Notice how he prayed over the people and the place, confessing his own sinfulness and lack of obedience. He took on a posture of dependency before God, asking God alone to intervene. This posture is crucial for us in ministry, because the needs are so great.

Also in the midst of that prayer he knew he needed to engage the community by talking to the most influential person in the area: the king. And what was the final thing he asked for? That he would be met with compassion. He took personal responsibility for the needs of the neighborhood. He became the answer to his own prayer.

3. *Never underestimate God's purposes* (2:1–8)

> I took up the wine and gave it to the king. Now I had not been sad in his presence. So the king said to me, "Why is your face sad though you are not sick? This is nothing but sadness of heart." Then I was very much afraid. I said to the king, "Let the king live forever. Why should my face not be sad when the city, the place of my fathers' tombs, lies desolate and its gates have been consumed by fire?" Then the king said to me, "What would you request?" So I prayed to the God of heaven. I said to the king, "If it please the king, and if your servant has found favor before you, send me to Judah, to the city of my fathers' tombs, that I may re-build it." Then the king said to me . . . "How long will your journey be, and when will you return?" So it pleased the king to send me, and I gave him a definite time. And I said to the king, "If it please the king, let letters be given me for the governors of the provinces beyond the River, that they may allow me to pass through until I come to Judah, and a letter to Asaph the keeper of the king's forest, that he may give me timber to make beams for the gates of the fortress which is by the temple, for the wall of the city and for the house to which I will go." And the king granted them to me because the good hand of my God was on me.

What Nehemiah did after his prayer was just as important as what he did during the prayer. He prayed, and in praying he was moved to action. He asked the king to let him go and see to the wall. And the king agreed. God answered Nehemiah's prayer. We must never let prayer for action be our excuse for inaction. As Nehemiah said, "Send me." That must be our prayer. God's answers to our prayers are often found directly through us. As is often quoted from Mahatma Gandhi, "Be the change you wish to see in the world." This shows us the power of a prayerful lifestyle.

We also see this in Matthew 9 where Jesus told us to pray that the Lord of the harvest would send out laborers. The harvest is plentiful; the workers are few. In God's great economy, as we cry out to Him in prayer for workers, we become the answer to that prayer. Certainly Nehemiah was that.

We need not use prayer as the idea, *Okay, we've prayed and now we're done. We can go on our way.* Too often it feels so overwhelming and we cry out, "It's so hard. There's too much to be done. What can we do?" But we can learn from Nehemiah's prayer: It set a fire *within him* to respond, and God called him out to do just that. There is a sense where God works in direct proportion to our prayerfulness.

It may seem overwhelming to initiate change in your community. I suspect the remnant in Jerusalem felt that way. Yet God's reputation is at stake in the way that we respond to broken places and broken people. It's important that we, as the church, understand the tragedy that *is* broken places. When we don't respond, the watching world ridicules us and God: "You really don't care; you really don't love us. You preach at us to get us saved, but you don't want to deeply engage in our messiness."

> GOD DELIGHTS TO WORK IN OUR MIDST IN WAYS THAT SEEM IMPOSSIBLE.

When it feels the most overwhelming, it's important to remember that God has purposes in mind—for Nehemiah, for His people, for Jerusalem, for the wall to be rebuilt, for watching nations in wonderment to see God work. Nehemiah could never imagine what God had planned to do. Broken places have been broken for a long time for a reason. Doing justice and acting compassionately is no small task. This story gives us hope that whether we're tackling broken walls on the South Side of Chicago or in Cairo or anywhere in between, we can be assured that God delights to work in our midst in ways that seem impossible. The reality is the work of God is often done by those who are often in way over their heads and yet have the audacity, the faith, and the courage to believe and to go forward. God granted Nehemiah favor and resources to accomplish the work that God intended to do; He can do the same for us.

4. Search out local needs (2:11–15)

> So I came to Jerusalem and . . . I arose in the night, I and a few men with me. . . . So I went out at night by the Valley Gate in the direction of the Dragon's Well and on to the Refuse Gate, inspecting the walls of Jerusalem which were broken down and its gates which were consumed by fire. Then I passed on to the Fountain Gate and the King's Pool, but there was no place for my mount to pass. So I went up at night by the ravine and inspected the wall. Then I entered the Valley Gate again and returned.

Nehemiah gathered a team together and "inspected" the wall. *Inspected* is used twice in this passage; it is a community analysis word, the same one we used earlier in the diagnostic formula for community analysis (in The "What"). Notice they went both to the resourced and under-resourced places (i.e., the fountain gate, as well as the refuse gate). Our efforts in the community must reach to both of those audiences. The leaders went to see for themselves the extent of the need—they got their hands dirty and personally experienced the brokenness, instead of delegating it to a committee. God, give us the courage and capacity to experience the need ourselves.

5. Pull others onto the team (2:17–3:32)

> I said to them, "You see the bad situation we are in, that Jerusalem is desolate and its gates burned by fire. Come, let us rebuild the wall of Jerusalem so that we will no longer be a reproach." I told them how the hand of my God had been favorable to me and

also about the king's words which he had spoken to me. Then
they said, "Let us arise and build." . . .

This passage reflects what each person did to help rebuild the
wall. This implies various talents, skills, and abilities that are inher-
ent in our churches as well. In fact we are told of one who *zealously*
repaired one section of the wall (3:20). Nehemiah gave them the
vision and empowered them to be part of the team, to get invested in
God's work. He reminded them of God's favor and ultimate success,
which brought encouragement to the team despite the obstacles.

In a sense Nehemiah told them, "This is embarrassing. We're
God's chosen people. The nations are watching and mocking."
Would it ever be that we, as Christ-followers, would be embarrassed
by our lack of activity in broken places? Could we weep and say,
"God, a watching world mocks and makes fun of our fear and our
lack of willingness to truly engage broken places for Jesus' sake." Nehemiah said, "No, we will not be a laughingstock any longer. We are
going to engage and rebuild this place. We can do this! God's hand
is favorable upon us. Let's arise and rebuild!" Nehemiah became a
recruiter, a motivator, a mobilizer. God, give us the kind of where-
withal to see the need, to cry out to others, tell the stories, and recruit
the broader body of Christ.

6. *Engage the community* (3:1–4:23)

Then Eliashib the high priest arose with his brothers the priests
and built the Sheep Gate; they consecrated it and hung its doors.
They consecrated the wall to the Tower of the Hundred and the
Tower of Hananel. Next to him the men of Jericho built, and next
to them Zaccur the son of Imri built. Now the sons of Hassenaah
built the Fish Gate. . . . Next to them Meremoth the son of Uriah
the son of Hakkoz made repairs. And next to him Meshullam
the son of Berechiah the son of Meshezabel made repairs. And
next to him Zadok the son of Baana also made repairs. . . . Joiada
the son of Paseah and Meshullam the son of Besodeiah repaired

the Old Gate; they laid its beams and hung its doors with its bolts and its bars. Next to them Melatiah the Gibeonite and Jadon the Meronothite, the men of Gibeon and of Mizpah, also made repairs for the official seat of the governor of the province beyond the River.... Next to him ... [and] next to him ... Next to them ... Next to them ... And next to him ... Between the upper room of the corner and the Sheep Gate the goldsmiths and the merchants carried out repairs.

The best way to reach a community is to engage that community. Just as we have to get other Christians on board, we must get the community on board as well. When they see that we're committed to the work, to seeking their welfare and peace, they will become more engaged and willing to get involved. These chapters are a beautiful picture of the specifics of the work. Over and over it says, "Next to ... next to ... next to" and "repairing ... repairing ... repairing." This was the work of bringing holistic ministry to a broken place. Repairing it spiritually, yes. But also repairing it socially, economically, physically, politically.

7. Courageously persist through opposition and fear (4:1–23; 6:1–19)

Now it came about that when Sanballat heard that we were rebuilding the wall, he became furious and very angry and mocked the Jews. He spoke in the presence of his brothers and the wealthy men of Samaria and said, "What are these feeble Jews doing? Are they going to restore it for themselves? Can they offer sacrifices? Can they finish in a day? Can they revive the stones from the dusty rubble even the burned ones?" Now Tobiah the Ammonite was near him and he said, "Even what they are building—if a fox should jump on it, he would break their stone wall down!" ... All of them conspired together to come and fight against Jerusalem and to cause a disturbance in it. But we prayed to our God, and because of them we set up a guard against them day and night.... I rose and spoke to the nobles, the officials and the rest of the people: "Do not be afraid of them; remember the Lord who is great and awesome, and fight for your brothers, your sons, your daughters, your wives and your houses." When our enemies heard that it was known to us, and that God had frustrated their plan, then all of us returned to the wall, each one to his work. From that day on, half of my servants carried on the work while half of them held the spears, the shields, the bows and the breastplates; and the captains were behind the whole house of Judah.

As Nehemiah and the community were working to rebuild the wall and bring peace to the people, others were criticizing, scheming, and calling for its demise. People taunted, opposed, and tried to demoralize Nehemiah and the team, yet they persisted. Nehemiah called the people to refocus their eyes on God and what He was calling them to do. Remember our God will fight for us (4:20).

When we begin to actively engage the community and seek its welfare, we will encounter deep, dark opposition. This is difficult, messy work to rebuild a place. But God calls us to keep our eyes focused on the work, the ministry, and to stay committed. Watchman Nee, a Chinese theologian, said, "Christianity is keeping one hand on the plow, while with the other wiping away the tears." We don't quit; we don't give in.

8. *Take time to celebrate accomplishments* (8:1–18)

All the people gathered as one man at the square which was in front of the Water Gate, and they asked Ezra the scribe to bring the book of the law of Moses which the LORD had given to Israel. Then Ezra the priest brought the law before the assembly of men, women and all who could listen with understanding. . . . He read from it . . . and all the people were attentive to the book of the law. . . . Then Ezra blessed the LORD the great God. And all the people answered, "Amen, Amen!" while lifting up their hands; then they bowed low and worshiped the LORD with their faces to

> the ground. . . . Then Nehemiah . . . said to them, "Go, eat of the
> fat, drink of the sweet, and send portions to him who has nothing
> prepared; for this day is holy to our Lord. Do not be grieved, for
> the joy of the LORD is your strength." . . . All the people went away
> to eat, to drink, to send portions and to celebrate a great festi-
> val, because they understood the words which had been made
> known to them.

Once the wall was rebuilt, the people gathered to worship the
Lord for His faithfulness to them. And then it was time to celebrate
their good work. We have much to be done, and in the midst of the
work, there is much drama. We can become so engaged in doing the
work that we don't pause to acknowledge and rejoice in God's blessing of the work that we've already accomplished. But it's important
to celebrate the small victories, to remember God's faithfulness.

9. *The world takes notice* (6:15–16)

> So the wall was completed on the twenty-fifth of *the month* Elul,
> in fifty-two days. When all our enemies heard of it, and all the
> nations surrounding us saw it, they lost their confidence; for they
> recognized that this work had been accomplished with the help
> of our God.

When we are committed to the place where people reside, when
we rebuild, the world takes notice. We engage in community analysis
before a watching world. The nations are all around us and our work
is a clear testimony to the power of God. They see the change, and
God is made famous in their midst.

SO WHAT?

Have you ever thought about Nehemiah's story as part of a "theology of place"? Read and meditate on Jeremiah 29:4–7. What opportunities did God give Israel during their time of exile? How might
this relate to a "theology of place" in community analysis?

APPLICATION

As you think about the importance of "the where" in your community, and how that may affect ministry opportunities, consider the following ways to gather information.

A. Explore the history and patterns of migration in your community.

Using what you have already learned through prayer-walking and ethnographic study (see examples in appendix 7), begin to collect information about the community narrative. Go to the local library, conduct Internet research, and continue first-person interviews to understand the history of the community, the patterns of migration in the area, population index as well as major components of society (politics, education, economics, health care, etc.).

B. Gather key leaders from the community as a focus group for identifying needs and roles.

Through the information you have already gathered, invite select leaders from the community who have valuable input into the community's welfare. Conduct a S.W.O.T. analysis (Strengths, Weaknesses, Opportunities, and Threats) with this task force. Take time to collect a small sample survey of their perceived wants, needs, hopes, and desires for the community, as well as how they feel they can contribute to the community's welfare. A final task may be to ask what questions they would like asked to better understand where they live and work. This will feed into a larger sample survey of the community.

C. Conduct a sample survey of an identified area.

Following the focus group, create a concise survey to be carried out for a brief time period (several weeks). Identify a few key areas that you would like the sample surveys to be distributed and implement the data collection period. After doing so, gather the data for analysis. At this point, if there is someone in your church or community who may be able to devote time to data analysis, that would be most helpful. If not, consider adding qualified people who would be able to interpret the data received from the surveys. Use the data collected to develop conclusions and recommendations for the church to implement or a church to be planted. Present the findings during a staff meeting or to a task force committee who have an interest in seeking the welfare of the community. (See appendices 3–5 for sample surveys.)

D. Develop a purpose statement for your involvement in the community.

What are your key activities? Based on the recommendations, what decisions must be made? What needs to happen in order to successfully carry out the purpose statement? Write down how you plan to show the community your purpose through specific and measurable steps.

E. Create a timeline of events.

What are your key objectives for the next six to twelve months? How can you break down your goals into manageable steps month by month? Identify the key people who will work with you and keep you accountable.

CASE STUDY: MULTISITE CAMPUS-BASED MINISTRY

In 2006 a group of committed believers and I planted Harvest Mission Community Church by the campus of Northwestern University in Evanston, a large suburb of Chicago. Our vision was to reach out to university communities in global cities with the gospel of Jesus Christ. After planting our church at Northwestern, our vision expanded into downtown Chicago and in 2008, we started a second site at the University of Illinois-Chicago (UIC).

College campuses are places of tremendous ministry need and potential. However, on many campuses, students are unengaged with the church. Christian ministry has been largely disconnected from churches. So our desire was to engage students in the context of a local church. Our congregation is made up primarily of students and young working professionals. In this context, we have tried to understand the spiritual needs and questions of young people.

I connected with Dr. John Fuder in 2010 to help me better understand our urban context in downtown Chicago. I joined a group of students from his community analysis class to survey students on campus, exploring their backgrounds, beliefs, and spiritual questions.

The results of our surveying were helpful in shaping our approach to ministry. First, they confirmed the diversity of our campus. We were overwhelmed by the wide range of the UIC students' religious beliefs and practices. From Islam to Hinduism to atheism, we realized that many challenges stood in the way of doing evangelism on our campus. Second, we saw potential ministry opportunities. Despite the challenges of diversity, we saw the need for a greater sense of community on campus. UIC was largely a commuter school so many students had no reason to stay on campus in the evenings or on weekends. We realized our church had to cast a compelling vision of a Christ-centered community that would address people's longing for deeper relationships. Beyond our Sunday worship service, small groups (what we call life groups) became the focal point of our ministry. We drove our entire ministry through these life groups. This allowed relationships to form organically to meet this great need on campus.

We also engaged the needs of the city beyond our campus. We started several mission projects to serve the poor and tangibly share Christ's love to our neighbors. We partnered with Dr. Fuder and Heart for the City to do several Urban Plunge projects. During the Urban Plunge, we surveyed neighborhoods and partnered with ministries and churches to do evangelism and service projects in their neighborhoods. Our church is part of a family of churches located on campuses throughout the world. Our partner churches from Austin, Texas, and Ann Arbor, Michigan, also sent missions teams to serve in Chicago throughout the year. These missions projects were a great way to disciple our members in response to the needs of our city.

Although we're still learning many lessons along the way, the principles of community analysis have been critical in helping engage the campus in our city.

JIMMY ROH
Lead Pastor, Harvest Mission Community Church
Chicago, Illinois

Chapter 6

THE "WHEN"

Q. *When is the time for community analysis?*
A. *Once we are willing to take the posture of a servant and humble ourselves to learn from and listen to our Lord and the needs of the community.*

When should we be engaged in community analysis? If you're like me, oftentimes I want to run in and try to fix something before I've taken the time to truly understand it. Let's fix it! Let's program it! Let's plant it! But in our enthusiasm we can miss an important part of the process.

Before starting a community analysis and rushing into practices, it is important to keep several biblical principles, or postures (attitudes), in mind. Our postures inform our practice. And those postures should be anchored in biblical principles.

A LOOK AT SCRIPTURE: IMPORTANT BIBLICAL PRINCIPLES WE NEED TO UNDERSTAND *FIRST*

To keep us from rushing in to "fix" our communities, first we need to focus on several important postures, along with Scriptures that reflect those postures. Only then can we successfully start any neighborhood mapping attempts.

1. *All postures must be gospel-centered.*

"[Jesus] said to them, 'Let us go somewhere else to the towns nearby, so that I may preach there also; for that is what I came for'" (Mark 1:38).

This passage is really a blueprint for us. First, Jesus engaged the community. In essence He spent Himself in the communities. If you go back through this first chapter of Mark, notice how many times the writer used the word *immediately*. Jesus was deeply engaged with others. He modeled for us that the call of the gospel is to give our lives away. Our calling is to glorify God. In many respects God asks us to read an audience and to dive in. It's nothing heroic; it's a simple response to the model of Christ.

> OUR COMMUNITIES MUST NOT SEE US AS RUNNING FROM BROKEN PLACES BUT RUNNING TO THEM.

You can move into a neighborhood, set up church, and start to preach at people—and some success may come. But to get to true kingdom life change, you must have a willingness to let your heart be broken with the things that break the heart of God.

The second thing that Jesus did was to energize or refuel Himself. In Mark 1:35, we read that "In the early morning, while it was still dark, Jesus got up, left the house, and went away to a secluded place, and was praying there." This wasn't about Jesus checking off His prayer list; this is more of Jesus quieting His heart and listening to God's marching orders for Him. We see Jesus model this pattern over and over. We need to spend that kind of time asking God what He wants for us in the community and asking Him to break our hearts for those people.

The third thing that Jesus modeled for us was to evangelize. He told His disciples, "Let us go . . . so that I may preach . . . for that is what I came for" (Mark 1:38). We advertise and try different strategies, but ultimately our job is to evangelize. We cannot lose sight of the main point of us being about the gospel.

The fourth thing that Jesus modeled was empathy. He had compassion for others, He suffered with them, He felt their anguish. This is the hallmark that we must be known for. Our credibility and authenticity is all about evangelizing and empathizing. Our communities must not see us as running from broken places but running to them—this is the essence of the gospel and the high calling of the church: proclamation coupled with demonstration.

The fifth thing that Jesus modeled was endurance or finishing the work He started. John 13:1 says that Jesus "loved them to the end." The work of exegeting a community is not something that happens overnight. We must be committed not to let up. We don't quit. We keep on.

The last thing is that Jesus equipped others. He taught and made disciples. In Acts 4:13 we learn that the impact of Peter and John's ministry was a direct result of "having been with Jesus." We do the same in our neighborhoods, which means we are deeply invested and committed to the people who live there.

The gospel of Jesus Christ stands at the center of community analysis. It is a form of worship, a vehicle for the church to honor God with our gifts and abilities and to reveal the love of Christ to a lost and hurting world. Community analysis becomes a valuable tool in continuing the work of evangelism and disciple-making as we learn and grow in our understanding of those outside the church building. As Dr. George Sweeting, former president of Moody Bible Institute, so aptly summarized: The main thing is to keep the main thing the main thing. There are many things we can do in ministry, but at the heart of it all must remain a holistic gospel message—word and deed. If the gospel does not remain the "main thing," we risk losing eternal kingdom impact in our humanitarian efforts.

2. All postures must be holistic.

"He has told you, O man, what is good; and what does the LORD require of you but to do justice, to love kindness, and to walk humbly with your God?" (Mic. 6:8).

Micah 6:8 has been my life verse for the last thirty plus years of ministry. That verse tells us to practice a lifestyle of compassion and justice, but that it all flows out of biblical righteousness. The Big Three (compassion, justice, and righteousness) are evident throughout Scripture. Jeremiah 9:24 tells us: "'Let him who boasts boast of this, that he understands and knows Me, that I am the LORD who exercises lovingkindness, justice and righteousness on earth; for I delight in these things,' declares the LORD." Want to delight the heart of God? Show your love for Him by practicing a lifestyle of justice and compassion.

The work of community analysis is not a new concept—Joseph, Moses, Nehemiah, Jesus, and Paul were all practitioners of community analysis who understood both their audience and the Holy Scriptures. They lived out God's mandate of justice and compassion for the marginalized in their society fueled by their knowledge of the Scriptures and love for God and neighbor. They can be an example to us today to know and love our neighbors. As we practically meet the needs of our community, we tangibly display the very same love of God.

3. All postures must be others-focused.

"The sons of Issachar, men who understood the times, with knowledge of what Israel should do" (1 Chron. 12:32).

The preceding verse is often used as a framework for understanding an audience. The sons of Issachar were a part of King David's mighty men. This group was comprised of warriors of great valor and strength, but those from Issachar were included because of their intuitive insight into the needs of that day. May God give us that kind of awareness to be culture-savvy. One of the great opportunities before us today is the interconnectedness of globalization: The nations are in our communities. In order to effectively reach them, we need to have a deep level of awareness about the cultures that are represented, because as diversity increases, so does religious pluralism. We see multiple layers of this playing out in our neighborhoods. It's humbling to ask others to be our teachers in order to better understand the place and the people. Yet that others-focused selflessness is key.

The focus of community analysis is the community. In order for the body of Christ to remain relevant in the cultures surrounding them, it is important that we learn who our neighbors are and the world in which they live. *Exegesis* is the theological term that describes drawing meaning from the scriptural text. In the same way we exegete the Bible, we must also study, or interpret, our context, our neighborhoods. It is easy to enter a community with preconceived notions of what we will find. The better posture is to look for and listen to those within the community who can help us clarify our own assumptions and misconceptions.

4. All postures must be dignifying.

"We carried on the work . . . so the wall was completed" (Neh. 4:21; 6:15).

Nehemiah worked with others to rebuild the wall around Jerusalem. The importance of this passage for us is that it was done in community. It was handled with the understanding that God has His players strategically deployed. This was an act of collaboration and partnership. We need to come to the realization that God has gone ahead of us and that those who are already in the community, who are struggling greatly under some of the needs there, are intricately deployed to be part of the solution.

> "HOW DO WE AFFIRM THE DIGNITY OF PEOPLE, MOTIVATE THEM, AND HELP THEM TAKE RESPONSIBILITY FOR THEIR OWN LIVES?"
> —John Perkins

In his book *Restoring At-Risk Communities*, Dr. John Perkins quotes a Chinese poem attributed to Lao Tzu, which demonstrates a unified approach to bringing change to a community from within as modeled in Nehemiah. "Go to the people, live among them, learn from them, love them, start with what they know, build on what they have: but the best leaders, when their task is done, the people will remark, 'We have done it ourselves.'"

Dr. Perkins, founder of the Christian Community Development Association (CCDA), asks a powerful question: "How do we affirm the dignity of people, motivate them, and help them take responsibility for their own lives?" Community analysis is in the business of transforming with the gospel not only individuals but families, communities, and social structures as well.

You may find that community analysis is a paradigm shift from the life and culture in your church. Or the principles of community analysis may already be ingrained in the DNA of your ministry. Wherever you land, it is imperative that you cover this process in prayer, humility, and courage. To neglect this posture is to run the risk of doing things for others that they could do for themselves. We often unwittingly organize programs to try and "fix" a broken place or people in need but do so at the harm of raising up leaders within the community who could, more adequately, help us not only to serve but empower the residents themselves to bring locally inspired change.

SO WHAT?

You may be wondering, *What's the big deal with emphasizing these postures?* But the reality is, our postures dictate our practices. The very foundation of our lives as Christ-followers, the way we will do community analysis and engage with our communities, is based on who we are. Our doing flows from our being. Once we understand these postures and are willing to apply them to our lives, then we know we are in a better place to move forward in mapping our neighborhoods.

APPLICATION

Before you start your community analysis, prepare your heart by reflecting on the following questions:

I. **Where are you?**

    A. Where is your church/organization spiritually?

        1. Are you praying for your community?

        2. Do you have a current evangelistic outreach strategy? If so, what is it?

        3. What Scriptures affirm your current strategy?

    B. Where is your church/organization geographically?

        1. Who are your neighbors?

        2. What is your understanding of their society (economically, politically, educationally, socially, physically, culturally, etc.)?

    C. What is your commitment level to this community analysis?

        1. Are you willing to recruit/mobilize leaders and volunteers to do the legwork?

        2. Will you commit to staying with the process for an extensive time period?

II. **Where do you want to go? What Scriptures affirm that?**

    A. What are the objectives for your community analysis?

    B. What are discoveries that can be made in a community analysis?

    C. Where do you want your church/organization to be?

        1. Spiritually (with the Lord)?

        2. Relationally (with each other)?

        3. Missionally (with the community)?

III. **How do you plan to get there?**

    A. What is your strategy to make this a reality?

    B. What is your timeline?

    C. Who from your church/organization will be leading?

CASE STUDY: LOCAL CHURCH OUTREACH IN ETHNICALLY AND ECONOMICALLY CHANGING NEIGHBORHOODS

Dolton, Lansing, and Park Forest are south suburban Chicago communities in transition ethnically and economically. They are characterized as collar suburbs and all have something of an urban look, feel, and life experience. Like many other churches around the world, our Chicago southland churches are challenged to be reconcilers across both racial and socioeconomic barriers. Therefore we've continually come together as a family to talk about our need to buck the tendency to move away, hear and heed God's calling to stay as the light of Christ, and be intentional about developing firsthand relationships in our communities. That led us to exegete our respective communities much the same way we seek for treasure in the Scriptures.

In the case of First Baptist Church of Lansing, through community analysis we discovered the common felt need for youth sports activities and learned about the differing perceptions about safety in our community (whites generally perceived the community as less safe than blacks and Hispanics viewed it). We were glad to hear that those who knew our church viewed us positively, especially through our children's programming. We were also surprised to meet several first generation Hispanics, whom we had not been prepared to survey. So that opened us to consider how we could best meet their needs as well.

Likewise, in the case of New Community Church in both Dolton and Park Forest, the greatest benefit of the team's work was the opportunity to listen, to hear personally from people living in our community but not necessarily attending our church. While the demographic data was helpful and suggested directions or ministries for us to develop, actually hearing from community members about their perception of the community and their perspective on community needs helped confirm or adjust our ideas for ministry development. For example, in the first assessment we knew from the census data that Dolton had a high percentage of single-parent (mostly women) homes. This was consistent with the felt needs expressed for day care, after-school programming, academic help, and tutoring.

However, when the survey results came back for Park Forest, along with the felt need for youth programming, which we expected, we also saw two areas we did not expect: financial counseling and job training. But both spoke to the community's declining economic base and socioeconomic transition for which Park Forest had been previously known. As a smaller congregation, we could offer little in regard to job training, though we culled information about places that were hiring and made that information known. We also offered financial management training through programs such as Financial Peace University, Crown Financial, and similar biblically based training programs that both met a need and gave us contact with people in the community who benefited from supportive relationships.

Youth activities, after-school programming, and child care were also high felt needs in Park Forest, but because of our church's location, we could not offer those programs as readily as at our campus in Dolton, which is across the street from a grade school, in the middle of a residential area, and on a main street through the village.

The report gave us a helpful snapshot of the village, and based on the information we gathered, we were able to consider various ideas for effective outreach and appropriate programming that we may not have otherwise considered.

As helpful as these discoveries were, we were most profoundly affected by the reality that our surveyed facts and figures came from real people directed to us by the Holy Spirit. This was no longer a project. Our hearts greatly expanded for our communities because now, this was personal.

MICHAEL EBERLY
Pastor, First Baptist Church
Lansing, Illinois

DANIEL GUTE
Pastor, New Community Church
Dolton and Park Forest, Illinois

Chapter 7

THE "HOW"

Q: *How do we do community analysis?*
A: *We do community analysis by networking service providers, finding neighborhood insiders, and identifying the needs of the broader community.*

Exegeting a community involves networking with other ministries and organizations that are also seeking to reach out to the community. It entails a deliberate pursuit of neighborhood insiders, individuals who can open doors into the lives of other residents. It also comprises gathering case studies and surveys to help us get to the needs in the neighborhood in order to find ways to serve the community.

I serve on the staff of Park Community Church in Chicago, which has recently opened a campus in the Rogers Park neighborhood. At the beginning stages, I spent time with the team training them in principles of community analysis, including surveying the area. Since we launched, we regularly pray and serve together with other local churches, schools, and social service organizations in the neighborhood. Insiders from the community consistently inform our activities and we are in the process of gathering case studies from the nations, which represent the diversity of our community.

A LOOK AT SCRIPTURE: NUMBERS 13:1–14:21

We can find a biblical blueprint for community analysis in the well-known story of the twelve Israelite spies who went to check out the land God had promised them. Throughout this story, we see a series of eight steps that I want to unpack to help us understand the clarity of what this looks like, and as we see that, we get a better sense of how to map a neighborhood.

1. Choose specific individuals

> The LORD spoke to Moses saying, "Send out for yourself men so that they may spy out the land of Canaan, which I am going to give to the sons of Israel; you shall send a man from each of their fathers' tribes, every one a leader among them." So Moses sent them from the wilderness of Paran at the command of the LORD, all of them men who were heads of the sons of Israel. (Num. 13:1–3)

God called Moses to send out spies from each of the tribes. The Scripture says, "At the command of the LORD." It's important to realize that we do ministry specifically at the command of the Lord. So Moses specifically chose twelve men and gave them their marching orders. It's important to see that God has a cadre of folks who are part of churches, schools, and ministries who could really be employed strategically to be involved. Too often we forget that. I think Hudson Taylor spoke well to this point when he said, "God's work done God's way will never lack God's supply." We have, in our own midst, skill sets that can help us. When we begin community analysis, we must choose wisely those who will be involved. Some of our choices have to do with gifting or talent. Some of these may be raw and need to be trained, but they are diamonds in the rough, so to speak. They have potential and are willing to have "on-the-job" learning.

Throughout my many years of ministry, specifically training ministry students, we have worked to engage the community with fear and trembling. There have been times when students have felt intimidated and said, "Doc, I don't think I can do this!" My response is always, "I'm learning with you guys." I have watched God go deeper with these men and women as they have grown in confidence.

2. Put together a survey team

These then were their names: from the tribe of Reuben, Shammua the son of Zaccur; from the tribe of Simeon, Shaphat the son of Hori; from the tribe of Judah, Caleb the son of Jephunneh; from the tribe of Issachar, Igal the son of Joseph; from the tribe of Ephraim, Hoshea the son of Nun; from the tribe of Benjamin, Palti the son of Raphu; from the tribe of Zebulun, Gaddiel the son of Sodi; from the tribe of Joseph, from the tribe of Manasseh, Gaddi the son of Susi; from the tribe of Dan, Ammiel the son of Gemalli; from the tribe of Asher, Sethur the son of Michael; from the tribe of Naphtali, Nahbi the son of Vophsi; from the tribe of Gad, Geuel the son of Machi. These are the names of the men whom Moses sent to spy out the land; but Moses called Hoshea the son of Nun, Joshua. (13:4–16)

It's amazing to me that we see all of their names. The ones we're most familiar with are Joshua and Caleb, but look at the specificity of God's Word to highlight the others. Moses knew the importance of teamwork. He may have called individuals, but then he put them together to work as a team. Leadership here is key. We really are no stronger than our team. Each of these names is of value to God. Our work is best utilized when we work together.

Oftentimes it's the Joshua and Caleb, the pastor and professor and missionary who get the publicity and the strokes of praise. But God's team includes the folks who may not get the recognition— those hidden saints who work behind the scenes, doing the heavy lifting of analyzing and listening to a neighborhood, trying to make sense out of it. They are doing the hard work of putting together the surveys and gathering the demographics, going up and down the streets and meeting with the different businesses, government officials, social services agencies, and other churches, and trying to understand all the information that is coming in. Each of these people have value and we need every one of them, because we cannot do this work alone.

3. Exegete the community

When Moses sent them to spy out the land of Canaan, he said to them, "Go up there into the Negev; then go up into the hill country. See what the land is like, and whether the people who live in it are strong or weak, whether they are few or many. How is the land in which they live, is it good or bad? And how are the cities in which they live, are they like open camps or with fortifications? How is the land, is it fat or lean? Are there trees in it or not? Make an effort then to get some of the fruit of the land." Now the time was the time of the first ripe grapes.

So they went up and spied out the land from the wilderness of Zin as far as Rehob, at Lebo-hamath. When they had gone up into the Negev, they came to Hebron where Ahiman, Sheshai and Talmai, the descendants of Anak were. (Now Hebron was built seven years before Zoan in Egypt.)

Then they came to the valley of Eshcol and from there cut down a branch with a single cluster of grapes; and they carried it on a pole between two men, with some of the pomegranates and the figs. That place was called the valley of Eshcol, because of the cluster which the sons of Israel cut down from there. (13:17–24)

Moses sent the team into the land to learn about it. He didn't take the Hebrews and barge in without doing the legwork and research first. What was the land like? What were the people like? We too must make an effort to discover who are in our neighborhoods. It's the people and the place. Evangelicals have often missed opportunities for ministry because we miss the significance of place (we touched on this in the "Where" section). God's heart beats for both. Obviously we're after the people—their souls are all that remains. But each of us is a by-product of the place we live.

I am a Dutch-German-American boy raised in a small Midwestern town. That's a part of me; it always will be. I spent my first seventeen years of life in Holland, Michigan. And the "learn" for me living in Latino, African-American, and other neighborhoods has been humbling. But it's crucial to really understand the people.

> TOO OFTEN WE GO OUT AND MEET SOMEBODY, TALK TO THEM, AND THEN THINK WE UNDERSTAND THE COMMUNITY AND ITS NEEDS.

Exegeting the community is about making an effort. This is going to be some hard work. You're going to have to roll up your sleeves and get dirty. It's going to cost and it's going to hurt. You have to get out of the ivory tower and into the trenches.

So much of my ministry experience with my wife in the early years with City Team Ministries was reaching out to young people, many of whom were involved in gangs, drugs, and sexual immorality. It was overwhelming because it felt as if they were thriving and the church had run away. I can assure you that when you get out of the building and move into need and brokenness, you will run into "the descendants of Anak" (v. 22), the big, bad guys. But this is where Christ calls us.

4. Report the findings

> When they returned from spying out the land, at the end of forty days, they proceeded to come to Moses and Aaron and to all the congregation of the sons of Israel in the wilderness of Paran, at Kadesh; and they brought back word to them and to all the congregation and showed them the fruit of the land. Thus they told him, and said, "We went in to the land where you sent us; and it certainly does flow with milk and honey, and this is its fruit. Nevertheless, the people who live in the land are strong, and

the cities are fortified and very large; and moreover, we saw the descendants of Anak there. Amalek is living in the land of the Negev and the Hittites and the Jebusites and the Amorites are living in the hill country, and the Canaanites are living by the sea and by the side of the Jordan." (13:25–29)

When the spies returned, they reported their findings to Moses. They recalled what the land was like, what the people were like, and their thoughts about the area. We too report and consider our findings. This allows us to get a sense of the scope of the needs.

Notice in verse 25, they had a specific time frame: forty days. Too often we go out and meet somebody, talk to them, and then think we understand the community and its needs. But that isn't the case. It takes time to analyze and get to know the depth of a neighborhood. Forty days to do neighborhood mapping is actually fairly minimal. Some suggest that we give it months, possibly even years, to really study a place.

5. Propose a strategy

Then Caleb quieted the people before Moses and said, "We should by all means go up and take possession of it, for we will surely overcome it." But the men who had gone up with him said, "We are not able to go up against the people, for they are too strong for us." So they gave out to the sons of Israel a bad report of the land which they had spied out, saying, "The land through which we have gone, in spying it out, is a land that devours its inhabitants; and all the people whom we saw in it are men of great size. There also we saw the Nephilim (the sons of Anak are part of the Nephilim); and we became like grasshoppers in our own sight, and so we were in their sight." (13:30–33)

The reality is that as you present the information, some will accept it eagerly. Others undoubtedly will be governed by fear. You know how it is when you get out of the building. Some folks will say, "It's never been done this way before"—the seven famous last words of the church! We fear what we don't understand, and so much of culture isn't wrong, it's just different. This may be a deep, long "learn" to get our people to understand.

Of the twelve spies, only two chose to see beyond the problems to the potential. They weren't naïve enough to believe it would be easy to take the land, but they also knew the opportunity—and that God had called them to that place. They chose to gaze at God and glance at the circumstances. This is what God calls us to do as well. We don't go out into a community believing that just because we've gotten to see the needs, the people will automatically accept us and allow us into the intimate place of their needs and problems. We still have to plan, to strategize. It may feel overwhelming, yet we can work, knowing God is on our side.

6. Negative reaction

> Then all the congregation lifted up their voices and cried, and the people wept that night. All the sons of Israel grumbled against Moses and Aaron; and the whole congregation said to them, "Would that we had died in the land of Egypt! Or would that we had died in this wilderness! Why is the LORD bringing us into this land, to fall by the sword? Our wives and our little ones will become plunder; would it not be better for us to return to Egypt?" So they said to one another, "Let us appoint a leader and return to Egypt." (14:1–4)

When the ministry opportunity seems overwhelming and impossible, it can become tempting to doubt and question whether God really called us to this place. Yet we must be careful when and why we decide to pull the plug of ministry. Is it because God has actually given us the okay to do that? Or are we so caught up in the problem and the circumstances that we don't rely on God to be with us, strengthening and leading us through the battle?

I can assure you that the more intentional you are about going out in the community, the more resistance you will meet—from the enemy, but also from the church.

7. Leaders response

Then Moses and Aaron fell on their faces in the presence of all the assembly of the congregation of the sons of Israel. Joshua the son of Nun and Caleb the son of Jephunneh, of those who had spied out the land, tore their clothes; and they spoke to all the congregation of the sons of Israel, saying, "The land which we passed through to spy out is an exceedingly good land. If the LORD is pleased with us, then He will bring us into this land and give it to us—a land which flows with milk and honey. Only do not rebel against the LORD; and do not fear the people of the land, for they will be our prey. Their protection has been removed from them, and the LORD is with us; do not fear them." But all the congregation said to stone them with stones. Then the glory of the LORD appeared in the tent of meeting to all the sons of Israel.

The LORD said to Moses, "How long will this people spurn Me? And how long will they not believe in Me, despite all the signs which I have performed in their midst? I will smite them with pestilence and dispossess them, and I will make you into a nation greater and mightier than they."

But Moses said to the LORD, "Then the Egyptians will hear of it, for by Your strength You brought up this people from their midst, and they will tell it to the inhabitants of this land. They have heard that You, O LORD, are in the midst of this people, for You, O LORD, are seen eye to eye, while Your cloud stands over them; and You go before them in a pillar of cloud by day and in a pillar of fire by night. Now if You slay this people as one man, then the nations who have heard of Your fame will say, 'Because the LORD could not bring this people into the land which He promised them by oath, therefore He slaughtered them in the wilderness.' But now, I pray, let the power of the Lord be great, just as You have declared, 'The LORD is slow to anger and abundant in lovingkindness, forgiving iniquity and transgression; but He will by no means clear the guilty, visiting the iniquity of the

> fathers on the children to the third and the fourth generations.'
> Pardon, I pray, the iniquity of this people according to the great-
> ness of Your lovingkindness, just as You also have forgiven this
> people, from Egypt even until now." (14:5–19)

Moses heard the complaints of the Hebrews and in response he prayed. He repented for the sins of his people, for their reluctance to get involved. He remembered God's promises and he battled for them, for the sake of his people, and most important, for the sake of God's glory.

I hope that we would come together with brokenness and tears and ask for God's forgiveness because we have run away from rather than toward the mission field. Do we really weep and repent over the loss of so many missional opportunities? God is bigger, what do we have to be afraid of?

> **IF YOUR CHURCH CLOSED ITS DOORS TOMORROW, WOULD YOUR NEIGHBORS EVEN NOTICE?**

8. *Ultimate result*

> So the LORD said, "I have pardoned them accord-
> ing to your word; but indeed, as I live, all the earth
> will be filled with the glory of the LORD." (14:20–21)

Ultimately we exegete a community and work to reach that community so that we bring our neighborhoods to Jesus, but also because we are committed to making God's name famous. We serve a mighty God, whose glory fills the earth. And the more we work on His behalf, the more the world sees that glory.

SO WHAT?

One of the greatest things you can do is for your life to model the ministry activities you are burdened for. So as you begin the process of more formally documenting the neighborhood mapping, be sure that you model what you want the ministry to be. Your motivation flows out of the model of your life, and in turn motivates others. So invite people to join you, at some level of ministry activity. Mother Teresa would always say, "Come and see." That's how she did her ministry and how she motivated others. *Come and see what I'm doing.* As you motivate, you will then need to mobilize people out of the expression of your life as you are there to serve. That begins more ministry. And from there you are called to maintain it.

In the times when it seems overwhelming or when we don't see a lot happening, we can understand that God desires for us to continue in the work to which He has called us.

Take an honest assessment of your church's—as well as the surrounding churches' and ministries'—relevance to the community. If your church closed its doors tomorrow, would your neighbors even notice? If they did notice, would they care? Or would they say, "Good riddance"?

In order to be serious about community analysis and to follow the blueprint of Scripture and "lead on our knees," we must become increasingly informed about our community. That starts with asking God to break our hearts, to give us compassion, and to provoke our spirits to want to make a change. Our rewards for this work is that the neighborhood becomes more peaceful and whole—and so do we.

APPLICATION

Following are the specifics on how to conduct community analysis, or neighborhood mapping. Though we've already covered some of these practices in earlier chapters, this section will give you a good sense of the timing and actual practice.

Network available resources

Take a look around the community to see if there are other churches or ministries who can help get involved in mapping the neighborhood? Is anyone else working with that audience? Can you partner with another church, ministry, social service agency, business, or schools? Others who are engaged to do good. With whom can you share and gather resources and information?

Once you find others, it may be helpful to approach them in a humble and teachable way and say, "We're new in the neighborhood and we're looking to find ways to join with your efforts in serving this community."

To help you become more conscious of other ministries and organizations in the community, ask them these questions.[1]

What is the context of this ministry?
What is the history of this ministry?
What are the programs of this ministry?
What is the structure of this ministry?
What are the costs of this ministry?
What is the implied theology for this ministry?
Who is this ministry trying to serve?
What are the skills present in this ministry?
What does this ministry do well? Leave undone?
What are the future possibilities for this ministry?

Most of these questions work for both Christian and non-Christian organizations. But they can serve as a guideline as you progress in partnering to do God's work.

Pick an insider

Identify an informant, or gatekeeper, who knows the history of the community and understands the culture and layout of the people groups who live and work in the area. This person may be a leader from a key organization, a longtime resident, or a government official. They know people and can open doors for you to become an insider. They are a model in the neighborhood. They may or may not be a Christian, but they have much to teach you.

> AN ACCEPTING AND INQUISITIVE POSTURE, WHILE BATHING EVERYTHING YOU DO IN PRAYER, CAN OPEN DOORS INTO ANOTHER CULTURE.

Our neighborhoods are filled with people like this, and they take great delight in sharing who they are and who and what the neighborhood is. We compliment and affirm them by wanting to hear their stories.

As you seek out that person, answer these questions to help guide you in your choice:

Who do I know in my community?

Where might I find someone who knows this community well?

Who are they? What is their role?

What is my plan to contact this person(s)?

How does this person's perspective represent the larger community?

Build a relationship with that person

As I noted in the "Top Ten Tips to Exegete a Culture" in the beginning of this book, we seek to become a part of our insider's world as much as we are able. Form a friendship and allow that individual to lead you to further discovery about the community.

Gather stories

After you've chosen that person, spend some time getting to know him or her. As the person begins to trust you more, conduct an ethnographic study. Researcher James Spradley explains ethnography as, "the work of describing a culture. The central aim of ethnography is to understand another way of life from the native point of view. ... Rather than studying people, ethnography seeks to learn from people."[2]

You can find specific questions laid out in appendix 1. As you "interview" this person, it is important to cover several categories in order to get a fuller picture. Those categories include life history, family/relationships, friendships/networks, interests/activities, and beliefs/values. You may also want to add other categories, depending on your specific needs. You may not always "stay on script," but it is helpful to work from an outline. And then be open to ask follow-up questions or dig deeper into their answers.

Be sure to approach this person as a learner. You are there to be taught, not to express your own thoughts, opinions, or beliefs. This requires humility, persistence, and the courage to push past your fears—particularly if the person is very different from you or your team. An accepting and inquisitive posture, while bathing everything you do in prayer, can open doors into another culture. For instance, let me reference another example provided by Haddon Anderson. Remembering the importance of going into the community as a learner, he asked his insider, "What are you good at? What do you like to do?" Haddon told me, "That man went from looking down and away while talking to making direct eye contact. He was excited to share about himself to someone who was interested and willing to listen."

As you actively listen with the intention of truly learning, you will discover aspects to the community that you may never have realized. But also, and so importantly, you give value to that person and to all the people in that community.

Survey the community

While the insider can go deep, you also need to hear from the rest of the community. Depending on the size of your neighborhood, you will need to determine if you want to do other ethnographies or surveys. Surveys give you a broader picture of felt needs and beliefs and are generally less intrusive. Appendices 2 and 3 offer sample survey questions as a starting point for your questionnaires. As a general rule you don't want to involve a person more than five to seven minutes. You want to lead them through the survey. It's far better to look them in the eyes, have the survey in hand, and walk them through it. If you hand them out or mail them, you probably won't get them back.

At the bare minimum, you want to get a hundred completed surveys in a defined community. If you can double or triple that number, the more data you'll have, of course, which means the more reliable your information. That takes time. So you also want to make sure the people you have administering the surveys are invested because most of these surveys will be given during a small window of time: Saturdays, Sundays, evenings.

Analyze your data

Depending on the formality of your community analysis, you will in all likelihood end up with some form of "field notes." A crucial step, often neglected, is to examine your data for holes, patterns, hooks. What missing pieces could your informant fill in? What interests, activities, or values are recurrent themes? Is there anything you could use to enter your informant's world more deeply?

What are the kinds of things you're specifically looking for in the data? I'd suggest three things: first, what are the common felt needs? As you see a commonality, you can begin to ask how you can run programs or build relationships in order to respond to those needs. Second, what are the basic worldviews that are playing out in the neighborhood? In some communities that are multicultural and diverse, you will have to explore audiences that hold multiple levels of belief sets. And third, what are people's attitudes toward church? And what are some ways the church could be more involved in the community? Those answers can lead to more specific questions about how the church could become more relevant and ways the neighborhood could benefit from having the local church there.

Filter your findings through a biblical worldview

What Scriptures speak to the information you are discovering? What does the Bible say about the activities, lifestyles, and beliefs you are exegeting in your neighborhood? What would the gospel look like in each person's life? What would Jesus do, or have you do, in response to the needs? A biblical framework is your strongest platform on which to mobilize your church/ministry/school to action.

Expand into the broader community

Your informant can act as a "culture broker" to give you entry into the additional lifestyles and subcultures within the broader community. As you become increasingly familiar with the people in your neighborhood, you can leverage those relational contacts into greater exposure and deeper familiarity with the needs in your area.

Present to your ministry what you've discovered

Put your surveys, data analysis, and ethnographies into a report and present that to your team or ministry, so they can "see" the bigger picture for the community. Ask the group to come to the meeting with open hearts and minds to what God may have you do outside the walls of your church.

Actively engage the community

You've done the difficult work of mapping your neighborhood. You gathered the surveys and ethnographies, put together a report, and presented it to the others in your church. With your newly acquired knowledge about your community, what do you do now? Plant a church? Start a new ministry? Refocus your current programs?

It benefits nothing and no one to do all the work and then let it sit untouched and undeveloped. And so you now must determine what God is calling you to do. You are now poised to do relevant, kingdom-building work in your community. Much of your response will depend upon your personnel and resources.

Look at different options for ministries, understanding that in order to reach the community spiritually, many times you first have to meet their needs, as Jesus modeled for us over and over. Does your neighborhood need job training? English as a Second Language classes? Financial training? Youth programs? What can your church do to work with the community to meet those needs? Decide and then move forward with compassion, commitment, and determination.

As you consider the direction your ministry needs to go after evaluating what the community needs, look at the questions you asked your partnering ministries and ask them of your own ministry:

What is the context of our ministry?
What is the history of our ministry?
What are the programs of our ministry?
What is the structure of our ministry?
What are the costs of our ministry?
What is the implied theology for our ministry?
Who is our ministry trying to serve?
What are the skills present in our ministry?

What does our ministry do well? Leave undone?
What are the future possibilities for our ministry?

With these answers you can build a bigger, broader ministry plan. You can offer practical suggestions for what the ministry would look like within the first year, then expand that to what the ministry would look like, or what you'd like to accomplish, in a three- to five-year plan, building in more analysis. And then from this information, ultimately, you can ask the question, "What do we see as God's agenda for this ministry moving forward in this neighborhood?"

Continually evaluate, study, explore

Our hope in Christ is firm, but everything and everyone around us is in constant motion. Is your neighborhood changing (again)? Who is God bringing to your community now? Is your church or ministry responsive to those opportunities? Are you making the connections in a relevant way or do you need to reassess your activities?

As our communities continue to reshape and change, we must continue to be active listeners and learners, understanding that our ministry may need to redefine itself. I suggest that we redo neighborhood mapping every three to five years (although five years is really the maximum amount of time to wait). We must always ask these questions, in every generation, in order to "serve the purpose of God" (Acts 13:36). It's work, but definitely worth the reward!

May God give you great favor, wisdom, direction, and deep humility as you learn your way in. May you discover the ways that God has already gone before you, and the ways in which you can truly scratch where the community is itching. And may the name of God be famous as a result of your endeavor.

CASE STUDY: ENGAGING A SUBURBAN CHURCH WITH LOCAL NEED

I live in Iowa where the church often adopts the well-known saying from the movie *Field of Dreams*, "If you build it, they will come." As a larger church, our modus operandi is attractional: come and see and get involved in our programming. That approach gives us access to pursue discipleship for many in our city, but not for all. That's where community analysis came in for us.

It all started with a seemingly simple conversation with our deacons, "Is our way of coming alongside the poor helpful or harmful? Is it enabling or developing?" Our discipleship of those outside our walls had become more about a transaction, and less about transformation. Something had to change.

We began to change the questions we were asking, studying the people who were coming, offering more counseling instead of compassion funding. Our leaders became students of our city, driving around with God's eyes to see the massive demographic shifts taking place. For example, nearly two hundred refugee families flood our city each year and inhabit ethnic pockets throughout. Something clicked. We needed to go to them.

We realized that more than ten countries are represented in a housing complex only fifteen minutes from our doorstep. Historically the darkest parts of our city are experiencing renewal as the nations are coming. Our approach, thanks to community analysis tools, has been to create platforms where relationships can take place. We began to offer neighborhood BBQs, backyard Bible clubs, soccer camps for refugee kids, tailgate parties—all legitimate expressions of the gospel as we seek to engage our city, get to know our neighbors, and take seriously God's command to love them.

All is well and good in theory, until something radical has to take place. Like Jesus in the incarnation, someone has to move in. I told the Lord in my seminary years that I would *never* do ministry in a city; I was too afraid, needed the respite the suburbs offer, and felt more equipped to do ministry among people like me. Community analysis, in the kindest sense of the term, has wrecked my world. While many are fleeing, God is calling my wife, kids, and me to the city—to aid our church in connecting with people who are disconnected from God. Apparently our elders heard the same thing, affirming that it is time for us to take the church into the city instead of waiting for the city to come into the church.

As our church has studied our city, we have had to face a lot in ourselves. We have had to let the gospel touch our innermost being as it roots out fear, prejudice, racism, and apathy. As we study the city, we recognize the massive implications of the gospel and that God is calling us to far more than what we typically see the church doing. The time is now. Being a church in the city is simply a matter of your location. Being a church *for* the city is about your vocation. I discovered an important part of ministry calls me to be a learner and become an insider—for the sake of my city and God's glory.

DOUG ROWLAND
Pastor, Outreach Ministries
Harvest Bible Chapel
Davenport, Iowa

THE LIFE HISTORY INTERVIEW[1]

The following questions can be a guideline for you as you form a life history of the individual with whom you are conducting an interview. Do not be bound by the subjects or order in which they are presented. Follow where you see the respondent's interest.

A. Family
1. Who is in the family? What is the order of their birth?
2. Can you describe a specific incident that would characterize your relationship to your parents? Your sisters and brothers?
3. What were the most important goals of your parents for themselves? For the family? For you? What are your goals for yourself? For your family?
4. What are some of the most memorable family occasions in your life? Describe what happened and why it is special to you.

B. Residence

 1. Where did you live? Tell me something about the place and the people.

 2. What are the most memorable places and events in your home and community?

 3. What kind of things happened at those places that are special to you?

C. Life Cycle

 1. When you were growing up, what events do you remember that were most satisfying to you; you achieved a goal, or something happened that pleased you very much?

 2. What happened on those special occasions? Who were the important people who helped make that happen? What meaning do these occasions have for you now?

 3. What events did your family observe in your life and in the life of others? i.e., deaths, marriage, births, etc.

 4. How did you and your family members participate in these events? What meaning did this have for you?

 5. Tell me your personal story! What were the key events in your life?

D. Community and Friends

 1. Who were special friends? How did you choose these people as friends?

 2. What made these people special for you? How did you help one another?

 3. How do you communicate with these people today, and about what subjects?

E. Beliefs

 1. What did you learn about gods? How did this relate to your family's interest?

 2. What does your family believe about God and the supernatural?

3. How does your family cope with illness and disaster?

4. What do you believe about God and about God's interest and concern about your life?

F. Questions of motivation primary to understanding meaning/action (This will help in your analysis of the life history material.)

1. What are your informant's most important goals over the span of their lives?

2. What are the key interests that preoccupy them at this point in time?

3. What are ordinary interests that compel your informant's attention, although not central to "goals"?

4. What interests are reflected in your informant's ordinary conversations? Daily routines?

5. How do informants order personal priorities as they relate to needs and goals?

G. Questions of motivation primary to understanding meaning/ action (This will help you in the application of ministry.)

1. What people and events have been most influential in helping your informant achieve goals and interests?

2. What message do you find in Scripture that addresses your informant's goals and interests?

3. What kind of relationship must you build to get your informant's interest and attention?

SURVEY BEST PRACTICES

GENERAL GUIDELINES

Begin with the "why?" Why are you asking these questions? Your answer to this question determines the purpose behind your survey and the questions you select or write yourselves. Remember that you want information of interest to your ministry. You want to be able to describe your community (i.e., age and gender). You also are interested in what your community sees as their needs (i.e., traffic violations or lack of job opportunities). Once you have this information, you can work out what those descriptions and needs look like in relation to each other.

Remember to have clear directions using basic terminology and very specific questions. A simple layout is necessary. There should be two sections. Demographics and Felt Needs. Place your demographic questions first, followed by your felt needs questions. Within the two sections make sure the questions listed meet these goals: least sensitive to most sensitive and fact oriented to opinion oriented. Feel free to follow our survey template as a way to get started. A short completion time requirement shows respect for your survey participants. As a general rule, try to keep your survey under fifteen questions.

GETTING STARTED

Now it's time to try your survey out (pilot testing). Make sure participants who fill out your survey fit the general demographic characteristics of your ministry environment's local radius. Time each trial run participant. Eight to ten minutes is the max. If trial run participants are struggling with reading comprehension, it will show up in how long it takes them to complete your survey. Unanswered questions can also teach us about cultural sensitivity. Lack of understanding or unintended insults can be minimized or fixed early on through a trial run.

REFINING YOUR SURVEY

Close-ended, neutral questions increase response rates. But these types of questions require good options for your survey participants to choose from. If several participants selected "Other" as an option and wrote in their response, consider including that option on your finalized survey. If several trial participants left a question unanswered, rephrasing the question or taking it out of your survey altogether may be necessary.

If what you expected to be a sensitive question resulted in only "safe" responses, then you are likely experiencing survey bias. The participants could be doing this for several reasons. They might want to present themselves in the best light possible to avoid violating the social norms of their community. An example of this would be no participant admitting to being divorced or currently separated from their spouse. Another important consideration is fear of judgment and performance anxiety. Most people want to be liked. Consequently, a participant might select answers that he or she thinks will please the survey distributor.

SAMPLE SURVEY QUESTIONS ACCORDING TO CATEGORY

You will want to tailor certain questions according to the demographic characteristics found in the United States Census data for your area of interest. A good rule of thumb is to have no more than six choices per close-ended question. Make the last choice "Other" so that the survey participant can fill in a more specific option if necessary.

GENERAL DEMOGRAPHIC

1. Approximate age
   a. 17 and under
   b. 18–19
   c. 20–29
   d. 30–39
   e. 40–49
   f. 50–59
   g. 60–69
   h. 70+

2. Profession or current occupation (please include student status)

    a. Full-time:_____

    b. Part-time:_____

    c. In-between work

    d. On government disability

3. Number of years in current occupation

    a. _____

4. Please select all of your ethnicities

    a. Black (Haitian, African, African-American)

    b. Chinese

    c. Cambodian

    d. Indian

    e. Japanese

    f. Korean

    g. Latino (Central/South America)

    h. Latino (Mexican)

    i. Native American

    j. Pakistani

    k. Spanish/Portuguese

    l. White (Caucasian)

    m. Vietnamese

    n. Hmong

    o. Other:_____

5. What language or languages do you speak very well?

    a. _____

    b. _____

    c. _____

6. How well do you read English?

    a. A few words (street signs)

    b. A few sentences (instructions)

    c. Many paragraphs (a newspaper article)

    d. Many pages (a fun book)

    e. Hundreds of pages (an academic book)

7. Which of the following best describes you?

    a. Agnostic (a god exists)

    b. Atheist (there is no god)

    c. Baha'ism

    d. Buddhist

    e. Christian Catholic

    f. Christian Evangelical

    g. Christian Orthodox Greek

    h. Christian Orthodox Russian

    i. Christian Protestant

    j. Confucianism

    k. Hindu

    l. Islamic (Sunni/Shia/Sufi)

    m. Jainism

    n. Jewish Conservative

    o. Jewish Orthodox

    p. Jewish Reconstructionism

    q. Jewish Reformed

    r. Jewish Renewalist

    s. Pagan

    t. Shamanism

    u. Sikhism

    v. Taoism

    w. Wiccan

    x. Other:_____

8. How long have you lived in your neighborhood?

    a. 1–2 years

    b. 3–5 years

    c. 6–10 years

    d. 11–15 years

    e. 15+ years

9. Relationship status
   a. Single and never married
   b. In an exclusive dating relationship
   c. In an open dating relationship
   d. First marriage
   e. Divorced/legally separated and currently single
   f. Divorced/legally separated and currently dating
   g. Divorced/legally separated and remarried
   h. Widowed/widower

10. How do you normally get around?
    a. Walk
    b. Bicycle
    c. Bus
    d. Train
    e. Car
    f. Taxi

11. How long does it take you to get from home to your work?
    a. 10 minutes or less
    b. 11–20 minutes
    c. 21–30 minutes
    d. 31–40 minutes
    e. 41–50 minutes
    f. 50+ minutes

12. What do you prefer to do with your social free time?
    a. Volunteer work
    b. Athletics
    c. Music
    d. Shop
    e. Movies/TV
    f. Online community
    g. Games
    h. The arts

i. Eat out

j. Other:_____

13. Do you think there is a universal truth?

a. Yes

b. No

c. Maybe

14. What is the origin of life?

a. Natural process

b. Personal creator

c. Impersonal creator

d. Don't know

15. I seek fulfillment through

a. Personal peace

b. Personal significance

c. Community belonging

d. Self-discipline

e. Security

f. Emotional support

g. Eternal hope

16. What do you think happens when you die?

a. Go to heaven or hell

b. Go to a level of paradise

c. Cease to exist

d. Reincarnated

e. Become one with the universe

f. Other:_____

SEXUAL MINORITY COMMUNITIES

1. Biological sex

a. Male

b. Female

c. Intersex (born with combination of male and female organs)

2. Sexual identity
    a. Male
    b. Female
    c. Androgynous (gender neutral)
    d. Pangender (switch back and forth between traditional gender identities)

3. Sexual affection or attraction
    a. Exclusively homosexual (gay or lesbian)
    b. Exclusively heterosexual (straight)
    c. Bisexual
    d. Asexual (no sexual attraction for others)

4. Relationship status[1]
    a. Currently single
    b. In an exclusive dating relationship
    c. In an open dating relationship
    d. First homosexual marriage
    e. First heterosexual marriage
    f. First legal union
    g. Divorced/legally separated and currently single
    h. Divorced/legally separated and currently dating
    i. Divorced/legally separated and remarried
    j. Divorced/legally separated and in a new legal union
    k. Widowed/widower

AFRICAN AMERICAN COMMUNITIES

1. Who is the primary caregiver in your household? (If it is you, please fill in whether you are the mother, father, brother.)
    a. Both birth parents
    b. Birth mother
    c. Birth father
    d. Grandparent(s)
    e. Extended family member
    f. Family friend

g. Sister

h. Brother

i. Me:_____

2. Including you, how many people are in your household?

　a. ____

3. "If I ran a ministry or church in my community, I would make sure it did these three things":

　a. Advocacy support for children and single parents

　b. Money management classes

　c. Evening church services

　d. Child care services

　e. Nutrition and cooking classes

　f. Sports programs

　g. After-school mentoring

　h. Music and arts programs

　i. Spiritual support groups

CARIBBEAN AND HAITIAN BLACK COMMUNITIES

1. "If I ran a ministry or church in my community, I would make sure it did these three things":

　a. Prayer for those afflicted by Rootwork (hexing, witchcraft, anxiety, stomach pain)

　b. Money management classes

　c. Sports programs

　d. After-school mentoring

　e. Music and arts programs

　f. Spiritual support groups

　g. Computer proficiency classes

　h. English as Second Language classes

　i. Career progression talks given by engineers, doctors, lawyers, and pastors

　j. Academic stress management programs

NATIVE AMERICAN COMMUNITIES

1. "If I ran a ministry or church in my community, I would make sure it did these three things":
   a. Prayer for those afflicted with ghost sickness (bad dreams, weakness, sense of suffocation)
   b. GED (General Education Development) mastery nongraded classes given in an apprenticeship style
   c. Spiritual support groups for alcohol dependency
   d. Equine Therapy (working with horses) for general mood disorders (depression)
   e. Cultural identity classes for adolescents (oral storytelling, tribal history)
   f. Tribal volunteer apprenticeship service trips led by certified technicians (plumbers, electricians)
   g. Domestic violence intervention programs
   h. Wilderness Bible camps

ASIAN AMERICAN COMMUNITIES

1. "If I ran a ministry or church in my community, I would make sure it did these three things":
   a. Prayer for those afflicted with spiritual maladies
   b. Academic stress management support groups
   c. Suicide support groups
   d. Parenting problem solving skills workshops
   e. English as Second Language classes
   f. Résumé development classes
   g. Career counseling
   h. Cultural identity preservation classes
   i. Elderly support ministries

HISPANIC/LATINO AMERICAN COMMUNITIES

1. "If I ran a ministry or church in my community, I would make sure it did these three things":

a. General Education Development evening classes

b. English as Second Language classes

c. Citizenship preparation classes

d. Apprenticeship skills programs for adolescents

e. Résumé development classes

f. Career counseling

g. Parenting problem solving skills workshops

h. Acculturation conflict management workshops given by a pastor

i. Suicide spiritual support groups for female adolescents

j. Child care services for single mothers

k. Intervening prayer for spiritual maladies (*nervios, susto, mal de ojo*)

ARAB AMERICANS

1. "If I ran a ministry in my community, I would make sure it did these three things":

a. Advocacy support groups for discrimination

b. Gender specific mentorship programs for adolescents (women mentor girls, men mentor boys)

c. Acculturation conflict management workshops given by a spiritual leader

d. Prayer and fasting support groups for stress management

e. Housing application assistance

f. Marriage enrichment classes given by a spiritual leader

COMMUNITY FELT NEEDS

1. What do you like best about your community?

a. Job opportunities

b. Public safety

c. Public transportation

d. Friendly police

e. Clean sidewalks

f. Housing

g. Nightlife

h. Education

2. What would you like to see done more in your community?

a. Street cleaning

b. Children activities

c. After-school learning events

d. Language classes

e. Day care

f. Citizenship classes

g. Money counseling

3. What is your biggest concern for your community?

a. Housing

b. Unemployment

c. Domestic violence

d. Gangs

e. School dropout rate

f. Drug and alcohol use

g. No sports programs

h. No citizenship classes

i. Public transportation

4. What is the biggest trouble for you?

a. Income level

b. Finding work

c. Transportation

d. Physical safety

e. Emotional safety

f. Drug use

g. Living conditions

h. Access to health care

FAITH-BASED

1. I enjoy reading, listening to music, or hearing talks about my faith
    a. Very regularly
    b. Somewhat regularly
    c. Rarely
    d. Never
    e. Do not know

2. I enjoy spending time with other people who share my faith beliefs
    a. Very regularly
    b. Somewhat regularly
    c. Rarely
    d. Never
    e. Do not know

3. I enjoy talking about my faith with others
    a. Very regularly
    b. Somewhat regularly
    c. Rarely
    d. Never
    e. Do not know

4. What makes it hard to go to faith-based activities?
    a. Work
    b. Transportation
    c. No activity is offered during free time
    d. No free time
    e. Don't like the environment the activity is held in
    f. Other:_____

5. The setting I prefer to learn or experience my faith
    a. By myself
    b. One-on-one meetings
    c. Small group

d. Classroom

e. Café or restaurant

f. Sports or athletic setting

g. Auditorium

6. "If I ran a ministry or church in my community, I would make sure it did these 3 things":

a. Parenting classes

b. English classes

c. Bible classes

d. Money management classes

e. Evening church services

f. Immigration assistance

g. Day care services

h. Nutrition and cooking classes

i. Sports programs

j. After-school tutoring

k. Music and arts programs

l. Addiction support groups

7. I want my local church to help with

a. Drug and alcohol abuse

b. Child education

c. Making the community look better

d. Domestic violence

e. Anger management

f. Parenting advice

g. Speaking English

8. Church people are

a. Polite

b. Helpful

c. Demanding

d. Withdrawn

e. I don't know any church people

9. If I went to a church, the reason would be
   a. To help my children
   b. Self-improvement
   c. Help for practical problems
   d. Meet good people
   e. Learn about the Bible

10. I would not attend a religious or faith-based event because
    a. Religion and faith is personal
    b. I had a bad experience before and don't want to try again
    c. I don't believe in God
    d. I'm always working
    e. I don't have available transportation

11. The time I would like to have community events

a. Monday:	7 a.m.–12 a.m.	12 a.m.–5 p.m.	5 p.m.–11 p.m.
b. Tuesday:	7 a.m.–12 a.m.	12 a.m.–5 p.m.	5 p.m.–11 p.m.
c. Wednesday:	7 a.m.–12 a.m.	12 a.m.–5 p.m.	5 p.m.–11 p.m.
d. Thursday:	7 a.m.–12 a.m.	12 a.m.–5 p.m.	5 p.m.–11 p.m.
e. Friday:	7 a.m.–12 a.m.	12 a.m.–5 p.m.	5 p.m.–11 p.m.
f. Saturday:	7 a.m.–12 a.m.	12 a.m.–5 p.m.	5 p.m.–11 p.m.
g. Sunday:	7 a.m.–12 a.m.	12 a.m.–5 p.m.	5 p.m.–11 p.m.

12. The best way to tell me about community events
    a. Posters
    b. Mail
    c. Website
    d. Email
    e. Radio

13. Do you find a spiritual element to life important?
    a. Very important
    b. Important
    c. Somewhat important
    d. Somewhat unimportant
    e. Unimportant

14. If you were facing a difficult time, how important would talking to a spiritual mentor/pastoral counselor be?

a. Very important

b. Important

c. Somewhat important

d. Somewhat unimportant

e. Unimportant

15. How important is it to you to receive spiritual support from a church?

a. Very important

b. Important

c. Somewhat important

d. Somewhat unimportant

e. Unimportant

16. At a worship service, I want the language to be in

a. English only

b. Spanish only

c. Both Spanish and English

17. Do you have a church or faith support group that you regularly attend?

a. Yes

b. No

LEARNING A NEIGHBORHOOD'S BELIEFS AND WORLDVIEWS

1. Gender
   A. Female
   B. Male

2. Age
   A. 18–25
   B. 26–34
   C. 35–45
   D. 46–55
   E. 56–62
   F. 63+

3. Marital Status
   A. Divorced
   B. Married
   C. Never married
   D. Separated
   E. Widowed

4. Number in household

    A. 1

    B. 2

    C. 3

    D. 4

    E. 5+

5. Race

    A. American Indian

    B. Asian/Pacific Islander

    C. White (not of Hispanic origin)

    D. Hispanic

    E. African-American (not of Hispanic origin)

    F. Other _____

6. Primary language

    A. Arabic

    B. Assyrian

    C. Chinese

    D. English

    E. Spanish

    F. Other

7. Sexual

    A. Bisexual

    B. Gay/Lesbian

    C. Heterosexual

    D. Other orientation _____

8. The human race is morally improving over time.

    Strongly disagree 1 2 3 4 5 6 7 *Strongly agree*

9. Everyone's perspective is equally truthful.

    Strongly disagree 1 2 3 4 5 6 7 *Strongly agree*

10. My life is a result of self-determination.

    Strongly disagree 1 2 3 4 5 6 7 *Strongly agree*

11. Science will provide an answer to most of the world's problems.
   Strongly disagree 1 2 3 4 5 6 7 *Strongly agree*

12. Which two categories best define you?
   A. Artistic
   B. Athletic
   C. Musical
   D. Philosophical
   E. Political
   F. Social
   G. Spiritual

13. Which one of the following best describes you?
   A. Buddhist
   B. Catholic
   C. Hindu
   D. Jewish
   E. Muslim
   F. Nonreligious
   G. Protestant
   H. Other

14. What do you think happens when a person dies?
   A. Reincarnation
   B. Purgatory
   C. Heaven or hell
   D. Cease to exist
   E. Nirvana
   F. Other

15. I hold my religious beliefs firmly.
   Strongly disagree 1 2 3 4 5 6 7 *Strongly agree*

16. There is absolute truth.
   Strongly disagree 1 2 3 4 5 6 7 *Strongly agree*

17. God exists.

Strongly disagree 1 2 3 4 5 6 7 *Strongly agree*

18. Jesus is God.

Strongly disagree 1 2 3 4 5 6 7 *Strongly agree*

19. There is more than one path to God.

Strongly disagree 1 2 3 4 5 6 7 *Strongly agree*

20. I know of a Christian church that is relevant to today's society.

Yes

No

If yes, please indicate the name of that church:

_____

FELT NEEDS OF A COMMUNITY AND THE ATTITUDES TOWARD THE CHURCH

1. Gender (This question is not to be asked):
   Male
   Female

2. Approximate age of interviewee (This question is not to be asked):
   20–29
   30–39
   40–49
   50–59
   60+

3. How long have you been living in this neighborhood?
   a. 2 years or less
   b. 3–5 years
   c. 6–10 years
   d. 11–15 years
   e. More than 16 years

4. What is your profession/occupation?

_____

5. What is your ethnic background?
   White
   Korean
   Black
   Chinese
   Hispanic
   Indian
   Mexican
   Pakistani
   Bosnian
   Cambodian
   Vietnamese
   Afro-American

6. What is your first language?

_____

7. How well do you feel that you are able to understand spoken
   English? (This question can be answered by the interviewer)
   Few words
   Few sentences
   Reasonably well
   Converse well
   Fluent

8. Would you be interested in meeting with someone who would
   help you to practice and improve your English?
   Yes
   No
   Maybe

9. Does your family have a religious preference?
   Buddhist

Hindu

Islamic

Jewish

Protestant

Roman Catholic

Other _____

10. How often do you attend church or other religious services?
Almost every week
Once a month
Twice a month
None

11. If you belong or have belonged to a church, why do you find it hard to go to church? What discourages you from going to church?

_____

12. If an opportunity was available, would you be interested in learning what the Bible has to say about who God is and how He relates to man?
Yes
No

13. If *yes*, which of the following settings would be most preferable to you?
a. Individually
b. With a small group
c. In a classroom type setting

14. If *no*, are there any other spiritual topics that you would be interested in learning about? If so, please specify:

15. In your opinion what are the two biggest problems in this neighborhood?
Abandonment
Gangs

School dropout

Crime

Safety

Poverty

Poor education

Domestic violence

Health care

Alcohol/drugs

Unemployment

16. Which of these areas would you be interested in? (Circle three important areas of interest.)

Sports camp

After-school kids' club

Movie nights

Parenting and family issues classes

Soul café (coffee shop)

Free immunization (provided by a medical clinic)

17. Would you like to give your name and address for future contact?

Name: _____

Address: _____

COLLEGE CAMPUSES

1. What is your gender?

2. What is your major at school?

3. What is your ethnicity?
   Caucasian
   Black/African-American
   Asian
   Hispanic/Latino
   Other

4. What is your first language?
   English
   Chinese
   Korean
   Japanese
   Spanish
   Other

5. Which of the following best describes you?

Buddhist

Ancestral worship

Confucian

Catholic

Protestant

Jewish

Muslim

Hindu

Other _____

6. If you are a Protestant, do you go to your home church?

7. Can you tell us why you do not go to your home church?

Because it is too far to go to my home church.

Because my home church does not have Sunday service for college students or young adults.

Because I do not have my old friends at my home church anymore.

Because I am not satisfied with my home church activities.

Other: _____

8. If you decided (or are thinking) to stop going to church, what are your reasons?

Too busy

Bad experience

Doesn't meet my needs

Don't know anyone

Other: _____

9. Which of these would be motivating factors to go to church as a Christian?

Training of children

Drawing closer to God

Finding forgiveness

Finding purpose to life

Meeting new friends

Other: _____

10. Please choose the three most important things in your life in
order of priority. (Please indicate 1, 2, 3.)

Money

Religion

Family

Friendship

Career

Health

Education

Other: _____

11. In your opinion, what are the two biggest problems of
Christianity? (Please indicate 1 and 2.)

Selfishness

Exclusiveness of other beliefs

Arrogance

Judgmental attitude

Lack of love

Lack of charity

None

Other: _____

12. I would be more fulfilled with more:

Inner contentment

Personal significance

Stability

Hope

Emotional support

Sense of belonging

Relevant beliefs

Purpose in life

13. Is there anything else you want to tell us?

14. Would you want us to contact you if we start any events?
Name:
Email:
Phone:

SAMPLE ETHNOGRAPHIES

ETHNOGRAPHY #1: A CASE STUDY OF CARLOS'S SEARCH FOR A BETTER LIFE[1]

The building vibrated with the strong beat of Latin music. The pale blue paint on the door was peeling. The ragged, old, brown carpet and the heavy window coverings made the apartment dark. As I stepped into the room, I could see the bare shoulders of a young man sitting in a wheelchair. The children, dressed only in diapers, stared at me with large black eyes. I had just entered Carlos's[2] "palace."

The furniture in the four rooms is sparse. The living room has a TV and a tattered couch and chair, probably pieces that were salvaged from a roadside dumpster. The narrow kitchen has a green plastic table and two chairs. One bedroom has only a full-size mattress laying on the floor. The other one is Carlos's room, stacked with his medical paraphernalia and some personal belongings.

He has a hospital bed that was provided by social services, a worn-out easy chair, and a computer on a metal stand. With all these things pushed against the walls, Carlos has room to maneuver his wheelchair in and out of the room. The closet has no doors and is stacked with all types of used equipment needed for Carlos's physical therapy three times a week. Four or five shirts hang amidst the mountain of metal and vinyl contraptions. He has a clipboard pinned to the wall where he keeps important notes and numbers that he slowly records with his uncertain left hand. His right hand still cannot grip to hold a pencil or even to offer a handshake.

Carlos wears black denim shorts and a large white brace around his torso. A half-full catheter bag hangs under his wheelchair and adds a slight smell of urine to the room. His dark black hair is cut short and all of his front top teeth are lined with silver caps. His voice is quiet and raspy. His long fingers are animated as he speaks, but his feet look withered and lifeless. With untrimmed toenails and chalky dry skin, they hang a few inches above the floor.

Four years ago, at the age of eighteen, Carlos left a dusty Mexican village that had few modern conveniences to find his fortune in America. Now he lives in this small brick duplex with his brother Francisco, his brother's girlfriend, Juanita, and the couple's two children, Mario and Maria.

I met Carlos through Juan, a Mexican man in my church. Even though Carlos's story is unique, many aspects of it mirror the path of the tens of thousands of Mexicans who come to our state every year.

LIFE IN MEXICO

Property is vitally important in Mexican villages. Without property, a person is destined to spend his life working someone else's land. Because the poor without property had virtually no way to improve their lot in life, many years ago the government instituted *el ejido*. Under this policy, the Mexican government seized portions of land and provided property to people who could never afford to buy their own. Carlos's grandfather obtained land through el ejido. He was allowed to divide his property among his children, but if his children did not claim their land by his death, it would transfer back into the government's hands. Carlos's uncle was a hard worker and a wise businessman and he developed his land effectively. Carlos's father was an alcoholic and he never even claimed his property. When Carlos was six, he moved with his parents and three brothers to a small plot of land that his uncle gave them. There they built a home. Their best hope was to attach themselves to this successful man.

This new life for Carlos's family began in the community of Ampliacion Balsa Larga, which literally translated is the amplification of or addition to Balsa Larga, the place of the "long raft." It was located outside a major city, but the new area was not a developed suburb. It was nothing but land—no running water, no electricity. Later as families built homes and became established, the government added these services. Eventually the Roman Catholic Church recognized the area as a parish and built a church; but for years, there was nothing but land. By American standards, Carlos grew up in very difficult conditions.

He remembers when the Catholic Church was built and he remembers his family being registered as part of the parish, but they did not attend church regularly. He also remembers their family being visited by the "Alleluias" (most probably Pentecostals), who also built a church in the village. They talked with his parents about God and Jesus. His parents never went to that church because the "Alleluias" used a different Bible and they did not believe in praying to the Virgin.

His parents insisted that Carlos go to the closest school, and he hated the classroom. As an elementary student he would sneak away from school and spend the day cutting sugar cane in the fields so he could make some money. When his father would find out that he was being a truant, he would put him back in school. Carlos completed six grades and then dropped out altogether. At age twelve, he worked in someone else's cornfields, day after day weeding the long rows of immature corn so that the stalks would not be choked out.

Carlos enjoyed his life. He was content to spend his days and his time off playing soccer with friends in the village. He did not think about leaving Ampliacion Balsa Larga for a better life. He was happy enough.

Then his older brother and several cousins left for America. The reports of quick employment and good pay ($7/hour) were enticing. He could work in the States for a few years and earn enough money to build a nice house in Mexico and buy a new truck. So Carlos went to see the "coyote," a man who would run the "chickens" across the border (illegally) for a fee.

Carlos was amazed when he came to the coyotes' community. They lived in big, beautifully furnished homes. They had nice new trucks parked in their driveways, and they wore expensive leather boots. The man Carlos talked with said he could take him to work in the Kentucky tobacco fields for a fee of $400. Since Carlos did not have money to put up front, the coyote allowed him to pay after he began his job in the States. With his heart racing from both fear and excitement, eighteen-year-old Carlos jumped in the truck.

LIFE IN AMERICA

The wages in the United States were great. Carlos paid off the coyote in less than a week. But the loneliness was horrible. Carlos missed his family and friends, and he was regularly calling his brother Francisco, who worked in another state. Within a short time, Francisco drove to get Carlos and bring him to his city.

Carlos did not drink, at least not before now. But his first night in his new surroundings, Francisco and his friends took him to a hotel bar and offered to buy him a beer. He agreed to try one. Before the evening was over, Carlos and his friends were drunk. When another group of Hispanics arrived, a knife fight broke out. The police were called and all but three of the men were taken to jail. Carlos and his brother somehow escaped the arrest.

Carlos got a job working with his brother at a chicken-processing plant. Several months later that work ended and they relocated again to another chicken plant. They switched states once more, where they met a Mexican man who let them live with him and found them work in a Chinese restaurant. When that work did not last, he put them in touch with a Cuban man who took them somewhere else.

They worked assembling mobile homes. It was hard labor, and Carlos was still miserable. He missed his home. He missed the food. He missed his friends. He missed the soccer games. He missed his life in Mexico. The only things he had in the United States were long weeks of work and short weekends of drinking.

More moves to more states, where he worked cutting boards at a lumberyard. That did not last, so he relocated to a place where he found a job working in the tobacco fields. The fields' owner provided a home for the Mexicans to live in. They would work the fields six days a week and he would take them into town on Saturdays to do their shopping. Carlos was back in the type of work he knew best and he liked the situation. He was making good money with little living expenses. He could finally enjoy a measure of prosperity. He bought new jeans, boots, shirts, and a stereo. And he had plenty of money for drinking.

But in time he became lonely again. The calls to his brother picked up and before long, Francisco was driving on bald tires to get his little brother. Carlos had agreed to buy him new tires if he would come get him. Finally, Carlos and Francisco decided to give our city a try. They agreed to drive a friend to the bus station, so they stayed to see what opportunities the bigger city held.

In no time they had a night cleaning job at a pork slaughterhouse. They moved into an apartment with two other Mexicans. Then they met four Mexican girls who had just crossed the border. They persuaded two of the girls to live with them, one of which was Carlos's cousin. Soon the girls had agreed to do all the cooking, in exchange for rent. This is a typical arrangement and it allowed the girls to pay their coyotes more quickly. They owed $700 each. The fee had increased significantly since Carlos had crossed the border two years before.

The men helped the girls get their "papers" so they could find jobs. These "papers" are falsified green cards and Social Security numbers. Carlos and Francisco found another job, working days in a chicken factory. Carlos was happier at this job than any yet, and Francisco met Juanita, the seventeen-year-old niece of the man who had been so helpful. Juanita had just come to the States and Francisco was helping her get adjusted. Their relationship quickly became romantic.

Our city was good to Carlos for more than two years. He did not tell his parents that he might not come back to Mexico after all. He liked his friends. He liked his job. He liked the money. He was even playing soccer on the weekends sometimes. And he was drinking too much.

LIFE IN A WHEELCHAIR

During the next two years, Carlos was arrested five times. His offenses were always either driving without a license or driving under the influence of alcohol. His jail sentences ranged from one month to two-and-a-half months. Even in prison he met other Mexicans who told their financial stories and offered him tips on how to better work the system.

Somehow his brother and his friends came up with the $400 bail, and Carlos was released from prison on December 27. He vowed he would not drink again. He fought to keep this promise for five days. Then late on New Year's Eve, he and a friend began to drink. They drank all through the next day. Sometime during the night of January 1, Carlos crawled in a van and fell asleep on the bench seat. His friend took the driver's seat and buckled himself in. That is all Carlos remembers.

Later he was told that his friend ran off the road and rolled the van. Carlos was thrown from the vehicle, and when he landed he broke his neck. A doctor was the first person to stop at the scene of the accident, and realized that Carlos was drowning in his own blood. He held Carlos's head so he could breathe until the paramedics arrived. The friend was treated for minor head injuries and released that same night. Carlos spent the next five months in the hospital.

While in the emergency room, Carlos was tormented by an awful dream. A scary man attempted to take him, along with a lady and a little girl, into a fire. He could feel the heat burning his body, but the man was never successful in pulling him in. The man kept getting frustrated that he could not get Carlos to die. Finally he gave up and left Carlos alone, even though his body was partially burned.

When Carlos regained consciousness, he could not move or speak. He had tubes coming in and out of his body. He was in pain and was terrified. They told Francisco that Carlos would be a quadriplegic if he survived.

Even though he did not realize it, Carlos had received a tracheotomy; therefore, he received all his nutrition intravenously. Day after day in the hospital, he wanted something to drink so badly he thought he would lose his mind. He would see nurses at the computer with cans of soda and try to think of ways he could get to the can, but he could not move. He would smell food and want to eat. In his mind he could hear himself screaming, "Please bring it to me!" but no sound would come out of his mouth.

He cried during the daytime because he was fearful and lonely, but Francisco came to see him every evening after work. Carlos lived for those visits. Francisco would always tell him that he would get better and encouraged him not to give up. Even though Carlos could not respond, he could hear every word.

Little by little Carlos began to get stronger. One day a Hispanic couple he did not know came to see him. They told him they were going to help him and prayed with him. Later they sent their pastor to visit him. This pastor continued to visit Carlos for the duration of his hospital stay.

Carlos went from one hospital floor to another as his condition improved. He began speaking again and amazingly began regaining some movement in his legs and arms. He was eventually moved to a rehabilitation center, and then six months later, he was released from the hospital. He has seen the doctor only twice since then. Life has not been easy since he left the hospital. Carlos has to wear diapers and he can do almost nothing for himself. Just recently he has begun to feed himself with his left hand and can even walk seven or eight steps with the aid of a walker.

Juanita found that feeding, bathing, and changing diapers for two children under three and for twenty-two-year-old Carlos was more than she could bear. She attempted suicide and was in a psychiatric hospital for seven days. My friend Juan and his wife kept Juanita's children, Mario and Maria, during this time, even though they did not know the family at all. In fact, they met as a result of the crisis.

The pastor who visited Carlos in the hospital is from the neighboring town. About six weeks ago he invited Carlos to a special service at the church. Carlos was able to ride in the van and attend the service. That night he trusted Jesus Christ as his Lord and Savior. And that is why he was able to greet me with a smile.

Every Sunday Carlos attends an English service in the morning at a church close by and someone from a Spanish-speaking church comes to get him for their evening service. He goes to an adult day-care facility three days a week to give Juanita a break; and a home health-care worker comes to assist him with physical therapy three times a week.

I asked Carlos if he still drinks. He said he has not had any alcohol since the accident and he never wants to drink again. Recently Francisco and Juanita had their two children baptized into the Roman Catholic Church. Carlos was encouraged to report that at the celebration following the baptism everyone drank—except him.

Carlos says he is happy. As I started to pick up the green plastic chair I had been sitting on to return it to the kitchen, I told Carlos, "When you left Mexico to come to America, your goal was to make money to build a house and to buy a truck. What is your goal now?" With a maturity in his eyes and a seriousness in his voice, Carlos replied, "I want to recuperate and get a job, so I can help my sixty-nine-year-old father who can no longer work, and I want to follow God's Word for the rest of my life."

MINISTRY RECOMMENDATIONS

1. Mexican workers and even their families are flooding to our state, and there are few Hispanic churches or ministries to help these

people. God loves them and we must be diligent about getting the good news of Jesus Christ to them, regardless of their motives for being here. Our church should move forward in launching our Hispanic church ministry within the next year (Matt. 28:16–20; Rom. 10:8–15; 1 Tim. 2:4–6).

2. An important part of this ministry will be welcoming Mexican newcomers to the area and helping them settle into a community during their first year here. Carlos's story illustrates the loneliness that often accompanies a move from one culture to another. Targeting newcomers will hopefully help them avoid some of the vices of drinking and partying; and offer them hope at a time when they are especially vulnerable. Hospitality is not a program; it is a love action. As we embrace it as individuals—bringing them into our homes and developing relationships with them—we will gain favor with them and have the privilege of sharing with them the claims of Christ (Rom. 12:9–13; Heb. 13:1–2).

3. This ministry must have physical assistance as one area of its primary focus. So many of the Hispanics in this area live in difficult situations. A true gospel ministry will demonstrate concern for physical needs as it ministers to the spiritual needs. We must be a reflection of God's heart for the poor and offer responsible assistance that meets real needs without destroying self-respect (Pss. 14:6; 140:12; Prov. 14:31; 29:7; Isa. 58:1–12; James 2:1–13).

4. This ministry must have an element of Hispanic leadership. The ability to communicate naturally in Spanish, along with an understanding of Mexican culture, will bring credibility to the church, rather than the ministry feeling like a white man's project to a different ethnic group. On the other hand, white people who are burdened for this ministry should be encouraged to participate and they should be equipped to become a part of the culture they are seeking to impact for Christ (1 Cor. 9:9–23).

PERSONAL LESSONS

Entering Carlos's world emphasized just how much I have been blessed materially. My wife and I are in the phase of life when many of our friends are moving into larger homes and making frequent comments about how they need more space. Our house looked like a mansion after spending the afternoon with Carlos and the four others who live in that duplex. I do not feel guilt about God's undeserved material blessing, but I do want to be a channel of sharing the wealth God has given me. I want to be a disburser, not an accumulator. Getting to know Carlos inside his world was an impacting part of the process that followed me back to the office and into my neighborhood.

Knowing Carlos has also brought color to the casts and statistics of my first ethnography. Some of what I learned from my research is now wrapped in emotion. I want my wife and kids to know Carlos. I want to maintain a relationship with this man, not because of research about Hispanics in my community but because I took the time to become his friend.

The factual research is important, but it took on depth of meaning as I became acquainted with a real person whose life contributed to those statistics. God forbid that my ministry and our church's future Hispanic ministry be shaped solely by cold information. May it be shaped by interaction with real people whose eyes and voices communicate the most important things—people whom God loves and who desperately need to hear of His saving grace.

You can walk away from ministry that is rooted in graphs and charts. It is very hard to walk away from Carlos.

ETHNOGRAPHY #2: A CASE STUDY OF ANNA[3]

I began my interview by assuring my informant, Anna, that the interview would be confidential, and I have not included her last name. I also informed her that if at any time a question was too probing or personal, she should feel free to decline to answer. I also told her that there were likely many areas where we would see things differently but that this was to be expected and she should not be concerned with offending me in any way. The purpose of the interview was for me to gather information about her culture and religion, and I was interested in learning more about both. She was very forthcoming and excited to share with me her life and her faith.

LIFE HISTORY

Anna was born in Karachi, Pakistan, and came to the United States when she was thirteen years old. Today she is twenty-eight. She speaks English and Urdu, she can read Arabic and also a little Spanish, which she learned while working in a doctor's office in our community, where she now lives with her husband and two-year-old son. When she moved to the United States, the first place she lived was in a neighboring state.

One of the things she misses least about Pakistan is the corruption of the government. What she misses most about her homeland is the friendly and warm environment of the neighbors and neighborhoods. The neighbors had open doors and lively interchange. Her neighbors were like her family and they were much less private and secluded than we are here in the United States.

One of her favorite memories is of the holiday called "Eid" (pronounced *aid*), which begins the day after Ramadan ends. It is the biggest holiday of the year, and it is a festive environment where the people wear new clothes and celebrate the end of a season of fasting, praying, and abstaining from sin.

FAMILY

Anna is the youngest of her four sisters and three brothers. Her oldest sister still lives in Pakistan and two of her brothers and parents now live nearby. The Pakistani culture and Muslim religion place a high value on honoring parents. One form this takes is in arranged marriages. It is considered an important duty and the responsibility of the parents to find a spouse for their male or female child.

Early marriage is a high value, primarily for the purpose of avoiding the sin of fornication. Most marriages are arranged and neither premarital sex nor divorce are considered options. There is no such thing as dating among the religiously devout. A man and woman cannot be alone together prior to marriage. Love is expected to develop after the marriage takes place but is not considered a reason to get married, although this is changing among younger people as their expectations are growing. In her family, there is still a choice regarding whether to marry but the pressure is to get married and most parents would not be pleased if a child remained single beyond the early twenties.

Anna and her husband now have a two-year-old boy and another baby on the way. I met them when they moved into an adjoining townhome shortly after they were married a little more than three years ago. They moved to the area to be near the mosque, which is within walking distance from our townhomes. There has been a tremendous influx of Muslims into the area since this mosque was built.

FRIENDSHIPS OR NETWORKS OR COMMUNITY

As observed earlier, family and community are extremely important in Anna's culture. Her parents and older brother live close so she sees them often. She is closest to her middle sister, who lives nearby, and her younger brother, who still lives in another state. Her in-laws often visit from Pakistan. Because her husband is very active in the mosque, they often have large gatherings of families and friends and a houseful of happily screaming children in the evenings!

They are also friendly with the Palestinian Muslim neighbors who recently moved into the building and from whom Anna gets Middle Eastern news via their satellite connection to Al Jazeera television.

INTERESTS AND ACTIVITIES

At this time, Anna is a stay-at-home mom but she seems discontent with her daily routine of cooking, cleaning, and child care. She has a bachelor's degree in graphic arts and would like to get a master's in early childhood education or child development or possibly go into nursing. She has an interest in doing something in terms of a future career, although she is unclear at this time regarding what specific direction that might take. Her husband is supportive of whatever she would like to pursue.

BELIEFS AND VALUES

Anna and her husband are devout Sunni Muslims. Sunni is the larger of the two sects of Islam, which comprises approximately 85–90 percent of all Muslims. The other is Shia, which is distinct because of its emphasis on the need for Muhammad's successors to be related to him and because they do not believe in the caliphate. Sunnis believe in the caliphate, which is the governing head of the worldwide Islamic community and practices rule by Shari'ah law.

Anna's morals and life decisions are based on both her culture and her Islamic belief system. She takes her religion very seriously, and unlike some Muslims whose faith is merely external, her faith is an expression of her internal convictions. For example, at about the age of twenty, she was the first in her family to choose to wear the head covering called the hijab. It was a difficult and awkward decision for her to make because it is uncommon within the American community. In addition, many of her Muslim relatives also saw it as unnecessary, but Anna felt personally convicted that it was important to her modesty, her values, and her spiritual growth. She explains that the hijab is worn to cover a woman's beauty and to help keep her from stumbling or temptation. It is also a way to appear less approachable to men and is a form of protection. Anna's faith teaches that a woman's beauty is reserved for her husband and family and that after puberty, only her brothers, father, and uncles should see her with her head uncovered.

In regard to prayer, Anna prays five times a day during given windows of time, not just because it is expected but because she desires to grow spiritually. She explains that each prayer begins with the same introduction each time and then continues with verses from the Koran that can vary as desired. The prayer begins with her hands in the air in an act of surrender, and then hands on the heart, and then a bow to the ground. This is repeated five times for each of the five daily prayers.

When I asked Anna to describe Allah, I must confess that I was surprised to hear her say that he is forgiving toward those who are trying to do what's right. She also pointed out that to continue to sin for this reason is unacceptable. This sounded similar to Paul's exhortation to Christians in Romans 6:1–2! When I tried to ascertain whether grace existed within Islam, she did not understand the question, but as I explained the concepts of grace as a free, unearned gift, she replied in the negative.

Anna believes heaven and hell are literal places and that one gets to heaven by believing that Allah is the one true god and that Muhammad is his messenger. Also, obeying his orders, avoiding sin, and doing good deeds, such as treating one's parents well, is essential. She cannot say with certainty that she can ever be "good enough" to get to heaven, but she believes Allah is forgiving and he loves seventy times more than a mother does. Even if someone is sent to hell, after they are punished they will be sent to heaven (which is surprisingly similar to the Catholic version of purgatory!). She believes Jesus was a prophet and that all the other prophets who came before Him were Allah's messengers. She also says that Muhammad suffered as Jesus did, for the spread of Islam.

When I asked her if she ever has questions about her faith, she says she questions a lot. One example is on the Qur'an's teaching about homosexuality. She says she had a cousin with whom she was close, but who was gay. Due to the inner conflict this caused him, he eventually committed suicide. Similar to many postmodern Christians today, she is conflicted about the idea that homosexuality has a biological origin as she was taught in her public school biology class, and the fact that homosexuality is forbidden by the Qur'an.

BIBLICAL VIEWPOINT

Acts 17:16

Just as Paul was distressed to see the city of Athens full of idols, my spirit grieves whenever I drive past the mosque in my neighborhood. When I think of or see all of the people who are held captive by the false teachings of Muhammad, I am truly burdened to pray for truth, salvation, and deliverance for my neighborhoods and all who enter there.

1 Peter 3:15

Christians are called upon always to be prepared to give an answer to everyone who asks the reason for the hope that we have. We must prepare ourselves to explain the points of attack or of questioning by Muslims (and others). The best tool we have toward this end is through the study of God's Word and apologetics. In addition, we are called to do this with gentleness and respect. One way for this to best happen is to begin by asking relevant questions, listening well, and establishing trust as the ethnography interview is an extremely valuable tool toward this end.

1 Corinthians 9:19–23

We must be willing to serve and affirm those we are trying to save. When Paul said in 1 Corinthians 9:22, "I have become all things to all men, so that I may by all means save some," I believe he was speaking of respecting and affirming the beliefs of others without compromising truth (as I have tried to practice here in a Muslim context). Paul seemed to search for the common nugget of truth upon which he agreed with those to whom he was ministering and to build upon that in order to point them toward Christ. Today we would call this "exegeting the community." Paul has taught us that information, common ground, and respect is a strong platform from which to share the love and truth of Jesus Christ.

Acts 17:1-4

Paul not only did his best to find common ground and even adapt to the community to which he preached, but in the case of the Jews, he reasoned with them from the Scriptures, which were common to both faiths in order to explain and prove that the Christ had to suffer and rise from the dead. There are also common Scriptures among Muslims and Christians in the Old Testament and in some cases it may be possible to reason with a Muslim from that point. For example, they believe in Moses and Abraham. Or even, beginning with their respect for Jesus as a prophet, to reason with them based on Jesus' own teaching from His biographies in the New Testament.

MINISTRY STRATEGY

I need to continue to build relationship and find areas of common belief, which open opportunities for discussing the similarities and differences in the belief systems between my Muslim neighbors and me. I have several avenues through which I can continue to reach out.

Since Anna stays home with her two-year-old son, I can stop by any time to visit. When I have him, I can bring my two-year-old grandson over to play or invite them to walk to the park. I can also invite her to lunch or to work out, both of which she has expressed a desire to do. I can also invite our Palestinian Muslim neighbor to join us. I can also look for opportunities to visit the mosque when it is opened to visitors as is sometimes the case.

I must reach out with areas of common ground. We share the common values of taking faith seriously, praying to God regularly, surrendering our will to God's will, desiring purity, avoiding sin, honoring our parents, and valuing children and family. We also share a common struggle within American secular society, which is hostile to all exclusive faith systems, including both Islam and Christianity. We can even explore some theological concepts and surprising points of similarity such as "God's forgiveness" and "God's love" with the ultimate goal of discussing how those diverge between the two faiths.

Most important, I must prepare myself from the Scriptures and in areas of apologetics in those essential points of difference between the Christian and Muslim faiths. Both knowledge of the Bible and books on the distinction between the faiths, such as *Answering Islam: The Crescent in Light of the Cross* by Norman L. Geisler and Abdul Saleeb, are good resources for preparation. Some primary examples of distinctions between the two faiths for which I should be prepared include:

- How Jesus embodies, both by justice and mercy, by giving His life so our sins can be forgiven (Rom. 6:23);

- How Christianity is the only faith with the concept of grace, which is an unearned and undeserved gift (Eph. 2:8–9; Titus 3:5);

- How God can be monotheistic but have a Trinitarian nature, which allows us to know God personally: God as sovereign over all (Father), God next to us (Jesus), and also God intimately alive inside us in the Holy Spirit (2 Cor. 13:14).

APPLICATION TO MINISTRY

This process has been an invaluable tool from which I have learned much. I realize the beliefs between my Muslim neighbors and me, though vast, do have some points of common ground from which we can converse. This tool has opened the door to build trust and a closer relationship where genuine conversations about faith and Jesus Christ can happen. In addition, by asking relevant questions and humbly listening, my Muslim friend has felt free to ask questions of me in return. In some cases these are questions she would not otherwise have considered, such as, "What is grace?" In other cases, they are common points of questions for which I must be prepared such as, "Don't Christians worship three Gods?" Or, "How can God die?" This process has removed my hesitancy to open the door to such conversations and any fear of offending; I have seen that beginning with questions and a genuine desire to learn is an approach to which people respond enthusiastically.

NOTES

Introduction: How Relevant Is Your Church?

1. Mark Van Houten, *God's Inner-City Address* (Grand Rapids: Zondervan, 1988), 21.
2. http://features.pewforum.org/religious-migration/destination-by-religion. php?sort=grandTotal.
3. http://www.migrationinformation.org/datahub/GCMM/Chicago-2005Datasheet.pdf.
4. http://esa.un.org/unpd/wup/pdf/WUP2011_Highlights.pdf.

Top Ten Tips to Exegete a Culture

1. John Fuder, *A Heart for the Community* (Chicago: Moody Publishers, 2009).
2. For more information, see Ralph Winter and Steve Hawthorne's book *Perspective on the World Christian Movement,* in which Brewster wrote a chapter.
3. James P. Spradley, *Participant Observation* (New York: Holt, Rinehart and Winston, 1980).
4. Marvin K. Mayers, *Christianity Confronts Culture: A Strategy for Cross-cultural Evangelism* (Grand Rapids: Zondervan, 1987).

The "What"

1. Jesus also shows the importance of observing a community. See Mark 6:34 and John 4:35.
2. Leith Anderson, *A Church for the 21st Century* (Minneapolis: Bethany Press, 1992).

The "Why"

1. Sheryl Montgomery Wingerd, "Insight Comes as They Walk the City," DAWN Report, March 2004.
2. Robert C. Linticum, *City of God, City of Satan* (Grand Rapids: Zondervan, 1991), 149–54.
3. For more information or to access the *Chicago Neighborhood Prayer Guide*, go to: www.h4tc.org/.
4. Margaret Clarkson, "Our Cities Cry to You, O God" (Carol Stream, IL: Hope Publishing, 1987). Used by permission.

The "Who"

1. Henri Nouwen, *Compassion* (New York: Doubleday, 1982), 4.
2. Henri Nouwen, *The Return of the Prodigal Son* (New York: Doubleday, 1994), 114.
3. John Fuder, *A Heart for the City* (Chicago: Moody Publishers, 1999).
4. John Fuder, *Training Students for Urban Ministry* (Eugene: Wiph and Stock, 2001).

The "Where"

1. Ray Bakke, *A Theology as Big as the City* (Downers Grove, IL: InterVarsity, 1997).

The "How"

1. Ray Bakke, "Together in the City" video series. Out of circulation.
2. James Spradley, *The Ethnographic Interview* (New York: Holt, Rinehart and Winston, 1979).

Appendix 1

1. Class notes from Dr. Sherwood Lingenfelter. Biola University, SICS 502, Social Organization, spring 1991.

Appendix 3

1. State law varies regarding the allowance for legal unions and marriages. All potential options have been included for your convenience. Be sure to verify your state's law to eliminate unnecessary and potentially inflammatory options for this survey question.

Appendix 7

1. This ethnography was written by a pastor in the southern part of the United States.
2. Names of individuals, the local church, and locations have been changed to provide confidentiality.
3. This ethnography was written by an American woman serving as a missionary.

ACKNOWLEDGMENTS

I would be remiss not to express my sincere thanks to a number of key people who helped bring this book to life.

First of all, Dr. Bud Hopkins, our much-beloved founding dean of the Moody Graduate School, now Moody Theological Seminary, where I was privileged to spend seventeen of the best years of my life. It was he who asked me to team-teach a Research Methods course, which over time became my own and was reborn as Community Analysis. Over the years hundreds and hundreds of Moody students have been trained to exegete their communities, and now as alums, they are scattered all over the world serving our Lord.

Some of the same students are currently being vetted as Heart for the City associates and in the past couple years have hosted Engage Weekends in their churches and cities across the United States and Canada, where initial drafts of the manuscript were used to equip their congregations. We even piloted the basic content of this book recently in Asia and in multiple countries in Africa! You certainly set in motion a great ministry chain of events with that class, Dr. Hopkins!

Numerous people helped take my course notes and shape and mold them into a book format. Jantzen Loza, my former faculty assistant and initial Heart for the City associate, taped and transcribed many of my teaching sessions and tirelessly worked his way through my "old school file folders" to produce the first draft.

Eric Hughes tediously poured over stacks of student community analysis projects and surveys to compile the sample questions in appendix 3. Elizabeth Koenig, my current project manager, typed and retyped multiple reiterations of the manual. And last but certainly not least, my editor, Ginger Kolbaba; the final draft would simply not be the same without you. Know that I am forever grateful. It would not have happened without all your hard work.

Deep appreciation and undying respect for the two men who did the foreword and the preface, Drs. Ray Bakke and Bob Lupton. You guys have lived and taught the principles of this book for decades—across America and around the globe! As mentors, friends, and colleagues, you have imprinted my life with these themes and I am indebted to your legacy.

Last, and certainly not least, to my dear wife of more than thirty years, Nel. You have put up with much change and transition in our lives the past few years, part of which has resulted in a lot more travel for me, teaching the principles in this book. You are still God's greatest gift to me and our family, and I love you with all my heart.

The late Chuck Colson said that if you want to change the culture, change the church. Bill Hybels often reminds us that the local church is the hope of the world. My constant prayer for this book is that it will serve as a catalyst to unleash the body of Christ to see and serve the nations right outside of its doors. May it be so, to the glory of our God and the courageous and compassionate impact of His people on our society.

Dr. John Fuder
Resource Global
Heart for the City

For additional case studies, ethnographies and surveys, please visit:
www.h4tc.org/resources

HEART FOR THE CITY

In this lively text, general editor Dr. John Fuder draws from the collective wisdom of God-centered men and women who are doing the work of ministry in the world-class city of Chicago; together they challenge us to action on behalf of our cities.

978-0-8024-9089-6

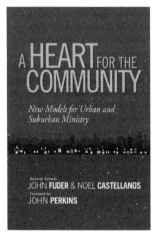

HEART FOR THE COMMUNITY

The Christian community is actively working to transform lives and restore communities throughout the city and suburbs. In *A Heart for the Community: New Models for Urban and Suburban Ministry*, you will be challenged by a collection of voices seeking community renewal. These individuals are involved in creative church planting initiatives, and they are serving the growing Hispanic and Muslim populations. Additional endeavors include serving racially changing communities, economic development strategies, and more.

978-0-8024-1068-9

Also available as an ebook

MOODY
PUBLISHERS

www.MoodyPublishers.com

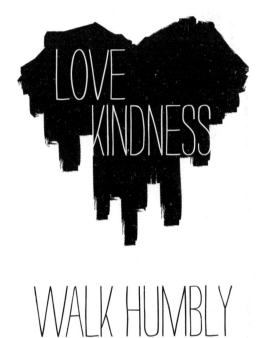

DO JUSTICE
LOVE KINDNESS
WALK HUMBLY WITH YOUR GOD

Heart for the City (HFTC) equips and empowers local churches for local service, instilling a passion for reaching out to and meeting the needs of the communities that those churches serve. By coming alongside church leadership in strategy and prayer, engaging congregations in the process of researching and truly understanding the needs of their community, and aligning resources with felt community needs, HFTC helps churches "bloom where they're planted." The HFTC model emerges out of decades of practical application of biblical missional principles to urban, cultural, and community ministry, encouraging churches to fully explore and realize God's heart for the communities where they were built. **Learn more at h4tc.org**
